John R. García

THANK GOD,
IT'S MONDAY!

Laity Exchange Books
Mark Gibbs, General Editor

Called to Holy Worldliness
by Richard J. Mouw

Christians with Secular Power
by Mark Gibbs

THANK GOD, IT'S MONDAY!

William E. Diehl

FORTRESS PRESS   Philadelphia

LAITY EXCHANGE BOOKS

To
Joshua, Rebecca,
David, Benjamin, and Amy

Second printing 1985

Library of Congress Cataloging in Publication Data

Diehl, William E.
    Thank God, it's Monday!

    (Laity exchange books)
    1. Laity. 2. Christian life—1960–
I. Title. II. Series.
BV4525.D49   1982   248.4'84133   81-71390
ISBN 0–8006–1656–1 (pbk.)   AACR2

1926D85   Printed in the United States of America   1-1656

Contents

Editor's Introduction

This series of *Laity Exchange Books* is intended to stimulate and to help the Christian laity in the exercise of their ministry today, particularly in the secular world outside the walls and structures of the institutional churches. It is therefore a great pleasure to introduce this book by William E. Diehl, for he is outstandingly qualified to write about "Monday-morning ministries."

Bill Diehl has had a strenuous and successful career as a major sales manager for the Bethlehem Steel Corporation, and he draws generously and frankly on these personal experiences. He is also a very loyal—yet questioning—member of the Lutheran Church in America. He is one of the founders of an innovative lay movement within that denomination, known as LAOS in Ministry. It is a special kind of laity fellowship, and he tells of some of its insights for affirming, sustaining, and developing lay people.

I find this book especially valuable because it raises some of the most awkward questions about Christian living in today's world: questions about power, status, competition, compromise, and financial security; questions about how large-scale organizations—secular or church—can become positively demonic in their demands upon us, and how we can and must resist them. Bill Diehl has written sharply yet wisely. This book will generate dozens of useful arguments and inform and inspire its readers.

MARK GIBBS

Preface

"Thank God, it's Friday!" Few American expressions are so universally shared. "Thank God, it's Friday!" says the tired businessman as he walks down the jetway from the DC-9 after a week of lengthy meetings, tough decisions, and little sleep. "Thank God, it's Friday!" sighs a young mother as she looks forward to a weekend of adult companionship after five days of changing diapers, cleaning food off the floor, and chasing after toddlers. "Thank God, it's Friday!" cheers the student after a steady stream of lectures, term papers, and exams. "Thank God, it's Friday!" mutters the grimy foundry worker as he leaves the noisy plant with lunch box in hand.

All over America, Friday is celebrated as a day of release. Bars and taprooms come alive at 5:00 P.M. on Fridays. Many private clubs feature T.G.I.F. parties with cut rates for drinks and perhaps a three-piece orchestra to help their members decompress.

For so many of us, Friday symbolizes at least a temporary relief from days of dull routine, hectic commuting, tough decisions, unpleasant working conditions, or emotional overload. Even for those who thoroughly enjoy what they are doing, the weekend becomes a welcomed change of pace. All of us need time to relax and renew ourselves after sustained periods of work. Indeed, we can give thanks that the weekend does provide that opportunity for us.

Then comes Monday. Have you ever heard someone say, "Thank God, it's Monday!"? What would cause anyone to make such a statement? For many of us, Monday signifies a return to tedium or stress, to dull routine or frightening uncertainty. The zest of the weekend fades into the "blues" of Monday.

Why aren't most of us eager to return to the Monday world? What do we reveal about our outlook on life if we are not happy with the prospect of spending five days at our place of occupation—whether it be an office, a home, a classroom, or a factory? Does it suggest that we do not see a purpose in what we do? Does it imply that we are somehow prisoners of a culture over which we have no control? Are we dominated by powers we do not even perceive or understand? Do we control the forces in our lives, or do they control us? What does this type of manic-depressive view of our week have to say about our understanding of life? Is the problem that on weekends we feel we can control the events of our lives, but on weekdays the events control us? Are we free on weekends and captives on weekdays?

It is the premise of this book that indeed we are held captive by many forces in our culture which we have failed to recognize. "Principalities and powers," the Bible calls them. The demands of our jobs, the values of our culture, the responsibilities of family and citizenship, and the uncertainties of life all press in upon us.

Are Christians any better able to cope with the pressures of the Monday world? Apparently not. There seems to be no noticeable difference between the way Christians and non-Christians face the Monday blues. In fact, for many Christians the Sunday worship experience represents the one hour of each week when they can completely escape the realities of the world about them.

Lord knows, we desperately need relief after the drudgery and stress of the week. We need to be healed by the power of the Holy Spirit. But is that all the Christian church offers—Band-Aids for the bruises of the past week? Is our congregating Sunday morning as the people of God simply for the purpose of licking our wounds and reminding ourselves that the travail of this world will someday be ended for us "in the sweet by-and-by"?

The church institutions themselves have inadvertently fallen into the trap of presenting the Sunday experience of worship as an end in itself. All the program planning, the sermon preparation, the choir rehearsals, the lesson plans, the usher schedules operate on the assumption that Sunday is the final day of the week—the culmination of all that has gone before. Yet our calendars show something else. Sunday is listed as the first day of the week—the beginning, not the end. When the early Christians shifted the day of worship from the last day of the week to the first in celebration of the day of

x

resurrection—of new life—they made a theological statement which
has largely been lost today. The gathering of the fellowship of Christian believers on the first day of the week was not an end in itself,
but a means to an end. For the church of that time had an outward-
moving mission. Sunday was not a day for escape; it was a day for
preparation.

Something is wrong. Does the gospel have no relevance to the
Monday world? Is it God's intention that we be freed from the
pressures of the world for only one hour each week? Do Christians
emerge from their Sunday morning gatherings with any greater sense
of purpose in life than those who sleep in until noon? Does the
Christian church do anything to help its people understand their lives
so that they can go into their Monday worlds with a sense of freedom?
Why is it that the "Easter people" are not of a mind to "Thank God,
it's Monday!"?

I am convinced that our laity desperately need help in connecting
their Sunday faith to their Monday world. Bible study and church
doctrine are of no help in the weekday world if lay people are unable
to make the connections.

The purpose of this book, then, is to examine the ways in which
modern "principalities and powers" control the lives of lay people,
and to show how the timeless message of the gospel and the witness of
the Scriptures can give us a sense of purpose in life and free us from
the captivity of our culture.

There really is nothing wrong with our sighing "Thank God, it's
Friday!" God knows only too well our need for rest and renewal.
What is troubling, however, is the evidence that the Christian laity are
not in touch with the way in which the gospel of Jesus Christ can free
them from the domination of contemporary principalities and powers
and give them a sense of purpose in life. If our God is truly the Lord of
all creation, we should be able to give him thanks for Mondays as well
as for Fridays.

PART ONE

THE WAY IT IS

1

Caught in the Middle

Martin

Martin is a state police officer in the criminal investigation unit of one of our large eastern states. His specialty is operating the polygraph, that is, giving lie-detector tests to criminal suspects. "I'm very good at it," he says in a quiet, assured way. "I've done this work for so many years that I have a very high degree of confidence in the accuracy of my tests."

We talked about how the polygraph operates and why he has such faith in its validity. "Still, I've got a kind of ethical problem," Martin added. "Legally, my responsibility is to administer the test and report my conclusions. But if it is apparent to me that a suspect is lying, what should I do? Should I use my knowledge to coax a confession out of this person, or should I remain noncommital?"

He went on. "Our judicial system is based on the assumption that everyone is innocent until proven guilty. The burden is upon the state to prove guilt. This can be a long and costly process, and the state can't always prove its case. When it fails to do so, a lawbreaker may go free. My supervisors are constantly pressuring me to conduct my tests in a way so that those who are lying will decide to make a confession of guilt. Obviously, we are not permitted to beat a confession out of a suspect, but I am often in a position where I can manipulate a person into making a confession and thereby surrender their right to a trial."

"How do you handle it?" I asked.

"Oh, God!" he said. "It's tough. After all these years, I still haven't worked out a solution. Sometimes, if a very serious crime has been committed and the suspect is obviously lying, I do work him

3

over a bit. I let him know that the tests are going badly by telling him exactly where he lied. Then I suggest that in his own best interests, a confession and plea of guilty might be best in the long run. On the other hand, if a crime is a minor one and the suspect is clearly telling lies, I'll say nothing and let the case go to trial. But I don't like having to decide by myself whether to try to manipulate a confession or not."

"Can't your superiors help?" I asked.

"Heck, no. All they want is to get as many confessions as possible. That way they look good and they have less trial work to deal with. They are a big part of my problem. They keep pressuring me for confessions."

Martin smiled and sighed. "On top of that, they have offered me a nice promotion to another kind of investigative work. They say it is in recognition of my good work, but I suspect they really want to bump me upstairs so that another, more cooperative, polygraph operator will take over who will get them more confessions."

"What does your wife say?" I asked.

"She feels I should take the promotion. We need the money, for one thing. But more than that, she would like to see me get out of the spot of having to make decisions involving whether or not to try to get confessions out of people. She knows how it upsets me."

"Oh, boy, Martin, that is a tough one," I sympathized.

"I guess if I'm really a Christian I should stay in this job and continue just as I have been doing. Because if I leave, the next person might try to get confessions out of everyone just to look good. And yet, I really don't know how my Christian faith relates to the problem. What do you think?"

Todd

Todd is a division manager for a large national electronics firm. Two years ago he received a promotion which involved moving his family from California to a large midwestern city. We were talking about a problem he now has with one of his closest associates, Arnie.

"When I accepted the job here as division manager, it was on the condition that Arnie could come along as one of my assistants. We work so well together, and I knew it would make my job so much easier to have him with me. It took a bit of doing to convince the company, and it took a lot more persuasion to convince Arnie. He and his family just didn't want to leave California to come here. I must say I didn't blame them for that. But I honestly felt it would be good for Arnie's career. So, after a fair amount of arm twisting, Arnie agreed to come along with me."

He continued, "Well, that was two years ago. Things have worked out very well here, and Arnie has been a super assistant. I've given him a lot of exposure to top management and, as I expected, his outstanding performance has been recognized. Two weeks ago Arnie was interviewed for a manager's job back in California. He is terribly excited about it. But it does present me with a problem."

"Because you don't want to lose him?" I asked.

"No, no. I wouldn't think of standing in his way. No, it's another kind of problem," Todd replied. "About six months ago, Arnie was hospitalized. Because of our close relationship, he confided in me about the situation. They had discovered cancer all through his body. Although he is receiving treatments for it and is back at work, the prognosis is not at all good."

Todd sighed. "I think more than anything else Arnie wants to go back to California in this new job so that if the worst happens, he will die there and his family will have better insurance benefits by virtue of his new position."

"So what's your involvement?" I asked.

"Before Arnie can get the promotion, I must submit a letter of total endorsement. The company does not know about his illness, and I think the situation is serious enough that they should. Arnie knows I must make a report on him, and he has asked me not to mention his illness. He is afraid he will not get the promotion if the company is aware of what he is undergoing, and I think he's right."

"I see," I replied. "So you don't know to whom you have the greater responsibility—to your friend Arnie or to the company."

"You got it," Todd said, shaking his head. "If only I hadn't pressed him to leave California in the first place, I'd feel better about reporting on his condition. But I'm the one who got him to leave there. Now he's afraid he's dying, and he wants me to help get him home. To do so, I must withhold information from my company."

"Todd, who have you talked to about this?" I asked.

"You are the first person I've confided in," he said. "I can't risk having the news get out."

"So you're all alone in this?"

"Yep. I've prayed for guidance, but I haven't received any clear signals yet. My report is due next Wednesday." He looked at me and smiled a bit. "What would you do?" he asked softly.

Kathy

Kathy, age thirty-two, is a working mother. She has a master's degree in chemistry. When her first child arrived seven years ago, she interrupted her brief career with a major petroleum company. Last year, due to financial pressures upon the family, Kathy returned to work.

"You know," she said, "it's incredible. No matter what I do, I end up feeling guilty and angry. During the years that I stayed home with David and Caroline, I kept thinking about all those years of college going to waste. Some of my former classmates were making fantastic progress in their professional careers, and there I was, washing diapers, picking up after little toddlers, and having absolutely no intellectual stimulation. I felt the world was passing me by. In so many different ways society kept telling me that what I was doing was not really important and that the real world was out there in business and industry."

"But now you *are* out there in what you call the real world," I reminded.

"Yes, and I still feel guilty and angry," she snapped. "I don't feel right every time I leave David and Caroline behind at that day care center on my way to work. It's a good center, but I know they cannot give my children the same degree of love and attention I gave them when I was home. I try to tell myself that I was with them in those important first years and that it's not how much time you spend with your children that counts, but the quality of that time. But I still feel guilty."

"How does Don feel about it?" I asked.

"Oh, he'd go along with whatever way I go," she answered. "He's supportive of me, as best he can be."

"What do you mean by that?"

"Well, I really need more than moral support. I'm still the one who prepares the meals after work, does the laundry, handles the shopping, and does most of the cleaning. Don will help me with some of the household chores, but he was raised in an environment where family duties were clearly defined. Much of the help I need involves what he considers women's work. He simply doesn't see how unevenly our family duties are divided. And I don't want to ruin our marriage by constantly nagging at him."

"And so you get angry inside."

"I really do," she admitted sadly.

"Well, must you work?" I asked.

"We do need the money," she said. "If we are to maintain our current standard of living and get our children educated, we must have a second source of income. Don's not pushing me to work, however. He's leaving it entirely up to me. But if I don't work, we'll have to cut back on things, and I'll be back with that old guilt feeling about not using my professional training."

"It's a no-win situation, isn't it?" I asked.

"Yes, it is. It really is," she sighed.

John

John has worked at the same drop-forge shop for twenty-two years.

"I hate every minute of it," he said very frankly.

"So why don't you quit?" I asked.

"Are you kidding? Where would I get a job that pays as well? I don't have any education. I need the money for the family, and the fringes are good. Hospitalization, vacation, insurance, and when I leave here someday, I'll have a half-decent pension. I can't get that any other place."

"Isn't there anything good about your job?" I asked.

"You tell me," he said. The shop is always hot and dirty. It is so noisy that OSHA makes us wear ear protectors. So you can't even talk to anyone. All day long I take forty-pound bars from a furnace, hold them under the drop hammer until they are forged into shape, and then drop them in a big tote box."

"What kind of product do you make?"

"I dunno," he replied. "It has something to do with the steering for trucks. But it goes through additional machining operations before the finished product comes out."

"Don't you have *any* variety in your work?" I asked.

"No, not really. Oh, we make different kinds of forgings, but they all look so much alike that I don't see much difference in them."

"Well, with all the years you've been there, weren't there any opportunities for advancement?"

"Yeah, they made me a foreman about ten years ago, but I didn't like it, and I asked to be put back on a hammer."

"Why?" I asked.

"I was always in the middle," John replied. "Management wanted me to boss the men and get more production out of them, and the men hated me because I stood up for management."

"Besides," he added, "there were many weeks when the guys on the hammers made more money than I did. They were on piece rate, and I was on straight salary. So there I was, taking garbage from everyone and earning less money. No way!"

"So, really, the only reason you stay is for the money and the benefits?"

"Sure," John answered, "what else is there?"

Judy

"I've got a problem," Judy said to me one evening as we were starting our dinner.

"Oh? What is it?" I asked.

"Frank McGrath has endorsed me for County Commissioner," she said.

"What? McGrath has?" I said in amazement.

"Yep. Today when I went to the Cementport Memorial Day luncheon, Frank was there making his usual long-winded speech. Part way through, he introduced me as a candidate for County Commissioner and told everybody to vote for me."

"I can't believe it," I said. "After all the times you've been critical of him. He knows you've never been one of his supporters. Why would he do this?"

"I don't know," Judy replied. "Perhaps he hopes that if he supports me, I'll give him support next time he runs."

"And will you?"

"Of course not. I can't stand him."

"Well, I'll be darned," I chuckled. "Frank carries a lot of weight in

Cementport. They love him. If he tells them to vote for you, they will."

"I know it," said Judy. "But I'm not sure I want to be endorsed by Frank McGrath. My friends know how much I disagree with his positions. What will they think of my integrity if I accept his support?"

"Yeah, but think how many votes you will lose if you repudiate his support," I said. "People in Cementport who might have voted for you anyway will be turned off if you do that to Frank."

"I know it. That's why I have a problem," she said.

"Of course, you didn't ask for his endorsement. He freely gave it."

"I know that," said Judy, "and you do, too. But who else will believe it? And if I don't intend to do him any favors in the future, shouldn't I tell him that now?"

"I can't believe this," I laughed. "We sit here complaining about political game playing in Washington, and here it is, right in our own laps. Well, what are you going to do?"

"I haven't decided yet," she replied. "What do you think I should do?"

Bob

Before we went into the room, Bob, my lawyer, gave me some last-minute instructions. "Remember, Bill," he said, "a deposition is merely a fact-finding exercise by the other side. We don't want to give them any more information than is necessary. The judge has authorized them to ask you only sixteen specific questions. I want you to answer them as honestly as you can, but also as simply as you can. Yes and no answers are ideal. Don't give them any free information. And if he asks you any questions other than the sixteen, I will not permit you to answer."

Thus began the preliminaries of a law suit in which one of our customers claimed that we had defaulted on a contract. Our company had engaged outside counsel to handle the case, and the attorney who was coaching me was one of the best in construction contract disputes.

"I've been in court against this guy before," Bob said. "He's not very smart, but I don't want to make things easy for him."

We entered the room. After some introductions and a bit of small talk the questions began—name, position, responsibilities, and so on. Part way through the deposition, the opposing lawyer asked, "From which of your steel mills did you ship fabricated materials to this job?"

I paused a moment and said, "None."

"None?" he asked in shock.

"Yes, none," I replied.

"But you admit you did supply steel for my client!" he demanded.

"Yes," I replied.

I looked over at Bob with a somewhat pained expression. He picked up my cue.

"Counselor, will you please excuse us for a moment?" he asked.

We stepped out of the room.

"What's the problem?" Bob asked.

"He's mixed up on his terminology. He asked from which mill we shipped to his client. The mill is where we melt and roll the steel. We shipped to his client from a fabricating shop. He should have asked from which shop we made the shipment. You said my answers should be precise and simple, so that's why I answered the way I did."

Bob giggled. "You answered the question exactly right," he said. "If he doesn't know how to phrase a question, that's his problem."

"But shouldn't we clear him up on his terminology?" I asked.

"We are not here to teach him. We are here to give specific answers to sixteen specific questions. You're behaving exactly right," he assured me. We went back into the room.

"Counselor," said Bob, "my client has answered your question factually."

The other attorney looked puzzled. "Mr. Diehl," he said, "on the one hand you have testified that your company furnished fabricated products to my client, and on the other hand you have denied that the shipments came from any of your mills. Will you please explain that contradiction?"

Bob's hand quickly shot out and rested on my forearm. "Don't answer that," he ordered.

"Why?" demanded the other attorney.

"Counselor," Bob said, "you have been granted permission by the court to ask sixteen specific questions. That is not one of the sixteen. I will not permit my client to respond to any additional questions."

"What!" screamed the other attorney. "He is contradicting himself. I have a right to demand clarification!"

"You have a right to ask sixteen specific questions. Please continue."

"You'll not permit him to clear up his contradictory testimony?" he demanded.

"Mr. Diehl has answered each of your questions honestly and precisely. If there appears to be a contradiction, that's your problem. Please proceed."

The attorney quickly completed the remaining questions, slammed his file into his briefcase, thanked me, and proceeded to leave without looking at Bob.

As we walked down the hall, Bob smiled. "You did fine. He's stupid. He never prepares his cases well."

"Yes, but on a point like terminology, what's wrong with straightening him out?" I asked. "If he had used the word *shop* instead of *mill*, I would have given him the answer. Sooner or later, he's going to get to that point anyway."

"Bill, I'm a good trial lawyer," said Bob. "A fundamental rule for me is never, never help the other side on anything unless it serves your own purposes. My job is to win cases for my clients."

I thought about that for a bit, and then asked, "Is justice really served if one side has a skillful lawyer and the other side has an incompetent one?"

Bob shrugged his shoulders. "My job is not to seek justice. My job is to win. The judge or jury is supposed to decide what is just. And if the other side has a poor counselor, I'd be negligent in my duty to my client if I didn't take advantage of that weakness. Your company hired me to win a case, not to be a nice guy."

The Problems Abound

Every one of the preceding accounts is true. With the exception of Judy, my wife, all the names and places have been changed, but I suspect the central characters of each story will recognize themselves and recall the conversations we had.

The stories are not unusual. They can all be replayed, with variations, by thousands of people. The polygraph operator's uneasiness about being pressured by his supervisors to manipulate people in order to make the department look good can be shared by many in all kinds of jobs. The division manager's struggle to decide to whom he was most responsible—to an individual or to an institution—is a daily event in thousands of jobs throughout our country. Kathy's feelings of guilt and anger are so common among women today that it is rare not to encounter it when we meet with a group of people.

How many workers see themselves locked into dull and dirty jobs simply because they feel they have neither the skill nor the courage to try something else? Is there anywhere in our political system where compromise or choosing the lesser of two evils is not the most frequent resolution of problems? In how many occupations is winning the ultimate and only objective?

Behind all these dramas lie deep and nagging doubts: "Am I right?" To be sure, humans have always had problems. The pages of history are filled with events which have profoundly affected the lives of millions of people. If we didn't have problems, we'd probably go out and think up some. Because we have been given the gift of free will, we have always had to make choices, and the options have not always been easy.

But it does seem that the dilemmas have been escalating. Modern technology has most certainly made the world smaller. The jet plane can place us anywhere in the world in a matter of hours, and the TV set can bring the world and all its problems into our living rooms instantaneously. The more the world shrinks, the more interrelated we all become. When the oil stops pumping in the Middle East, the lines start forming at the gas pumps in our Midwest. When a new steel mill goes on stream at Ohgishima, Japan, an old one is knocked out of the game in Youngstown, Ohio or Liverpool, England.

More scientific developments have come in the past fifty years than in all of previously recorded time. We have sent people to the moon and back. We are in the midst of an explosion of computer technology so profound that some futurists predict it will have greater impact on civilization than our discovery of how to read and write. Although we have already become accustomed to such biomedical feats as organ transplants, test-tube babies, and genetic manipulation, we are told that we are merely on the threshold of discovery in this field. The ethical implications of such scientific discoveries boggle the mind.

In the industrially developed countries, especially North America, the post-World War II years have brought an affluence to most of our people which would never have been dreamed of at the opening of this century. Two cars in every driveway, a second vacation home, a trip to Europe, a recreational vehicle, a boat, stereo hi-fi, TV with video-tapes, microwave ovens, home freezers, home movies—the list of nonessential "goodies" within the reach of most of our citizens is staggering. Yet we are aware and are uneasy that in other parts of the world people still go without the basics of food, clothing, and shelter.

We try to manage the growing complexities of life only to encounter more frustrations. As we try to control the growth of population around the world, strong ethical, moral, and religious issues are raised. As we pass laws to lessen the polluting effects of our indus-trialized society, we find that some plants are forced to close. As we try to deal with inequalities of opportunity or maldistribution of wealth, the issue of a "free society versus a controlled society" moves on stage.

Over all these developments and issues, like the sword of Damo-cles, hangs that unspeakable possibility: a nuclear holocaust—so incredibly frightening that it is the issue we most want to flee from. We play games of "nuclear equivalency" as if we were talking about snowballs. As more nations get the bomb, the ultimate likelihood of its use becomes more certain. A recent poll showed that a majority of Americans now believe that there will someday be a major war involving nuclear weaponry. And yet we are swept onward in a spiral of escalating armaments with no one really knowing how to reverse the drift of events.

The complexity of the problems we face today surpasses any previous time in history. Whoever said, "You cannot do just one thing" was absolutely right. Every action we take and every decision we make affects someone else for good or for bad.

Is it any wonder that we sigh, "Thank God, it's Friday!"?

Principalities and Powers

The most frustrating aspect of trying to deal with the complexities of our world today is the nagging suspicion that we have no control over our lives. We are reacting to events rather than managing them. We seem unable to identify and deal with the forces which often carry us in a direction we do not want to go. For example, while we are convinced that no one in this world wants a nuclear holocaust, we cannot change the apparent drift toward one. While all of us want to eliminate hunger, we can't seem to get a handle on a way of doing it.

At a more personal level, we find ourselves caught in dilemmas from which there does not seem to be a clear way out. The system gives us only limited choices, and so, regrettably, we have to pick the lesser of two evils. Martin, Todd, Kathy, and the others are all trapped in no-win situations. Why should this be so?

In *An Ethic for Christians and Other Aliens in a Strange Land,*[1] William Stringfellow discusses the biblical concept of "principalities and powers." The New Testament uses these terms in Rom. 8:38, Eph. 1:21 and 6:12, Col. 2:15, and Titus 3:1, although some of the newer translations may have slightly different words. The New English Bible refers to "spirits or superhuman powers" and "cosmic powers and authorities." At some points the J. B. Phillips paraphrase elects to use the words "organizations and powers," while Today's English Version (*Good News Bible*) favors the terms "spiritual forces and authorities" in most instances.

Stringfellow defines "principalities and powers" as organizations, institutions, movements, or ideologies. He would, therefore, include such institutions or organizations as IBM, Bethlehem Steel, the Lutheran Church in America and other churches, Yale University, the Ford Foundation, the Teamsters' Union, and the U.S. Government as principalities. Also included would be such movements as the NAACP, the Ku Klux Klan, The National Organization for Women, the Moral Majority, and the Sierra Club. Finally, he would include such ideologies as capitalism, socialism, astrology, humanism, scientism, patriotism, and many more. Obviously, then, modern principalities and powers *are* legion.

These principalities and powers take on a being of their own, "having their own existence, personality, and mode of life."[2] Stringfellow is surprised that we fail to recognize this fact, particularly since the principalities and powers seek to dominate human beings. Moreover, because institutions, movements, and ideologies are the creations of human beings, they automatically assume the imperfect nature of humans. Theoretically they may have been created to serve humans, but in their fallen nature they move toward possessing people and thereby become demonic in nature. "The gravest effort of the principalities is the capture of humans in their service."[3]

Americans are incredibly naive in assuming that these principalities and powers are benign. They are not. Frequently they are out to dominate humans, and "human beings do not readily recognize their victim status in relation to the principalities."[4] The more one serves these modern day principalities and powers, the more one is a captive of them.

> The American problem is not so simple that it can be attributed to a few—or even many—evil men in high places, any more than it can be blamed on long-haired youth or a handful of black revolutionaries. Besides, men in high places are not exceptionally immoral; they are, on the contrary, quite ordinarily moral. In truth, the conspicuous moral fact about our generals, our industrialists, our scientists, our commercial and political leaders is that they are the most obvious and pathetic prisoners in American society. There is unleashed among the principalities in this society a ruthless, self-proliferating, all-consuming institutional process which assaults, dispirits, defeats and destroys human life even among, and *primarily* among, those persons in positions of institutional leadership. They are left with titles, but without effectual authority; with the trappings of power, but without control over the institutions they head; in nominal command, but bereft of dominion. These same principalities, as has been mentioned, threaten and defy and enslave human beings of other status in diverse ways, but the most poignant victim of the demonic in America today is the so-called leader.[5]

The relationships between principalities and human beings "are more intricate, more complicated, more ambiguous, more tense, more hectic than words can describe. The milieu of the powers and principalities *is* chaos."[6]

John Howard Yoder reminds us, however, that principalities and powers are part of God's grand creation.[7] In Col. 1:16, for example, Paul writes, "In him [Christ] were created all things, those in heaven and those on earth, visible and invisible, whether thrones or dominions or principalities or powers; all was created through him and by him."

Although principalities and powers are part of God's creation, like man they have rebelled and are fallen. Yet they are not totally without purpose. They provide the structure for society so that *we cannot live without them*. At the same time, however, they do not and cannot enable people "to live a genuinely free, human, loving life." Instead, they absolutize themselves and demand unconditional loyalty from us. They harm and enslave us. Therefore, *we cannot live with them.*

Yoder points out that Jesus, by living a genuinely free and human existence among humankind, broke the sovereignty of these powers in his life. Not even to save his own life would he let himself be made a slave of these powers. So, Paul writes, "he [God] disarmed the principalities and powers and made a public example of them, triumphing over them in him [Christ]" (Col. 2:15).

The writings of Stringfellow, Yoder, and others on the subject of a contemporary understanding of "principalities and powers" have been very helpful to me. The concept provides the basis for a practical and theological understanding of our current situation. I agree with these writers that it is tragic the church has tended to overlook this important biblical teaching.

The Bible has other concepts which will be helpful in dealing with our current situation. Before we go further with the development of our biblical and theological positions, however, it seems necessary that we follow Stringfellow's admonition to examine carefully our contemporary principalities and powers in order to see more clearly the intricate, subtle, and at times devastating ways in which they take over our lives.

Let's start with just one example—with an ideology which seems to be universally accepted, but which has blossomed in all its fullness in America. Let's take a look at competition.

NOTES—CHAPTER 1

1. William Stringfellow, *An Ethic for Christians and Other Aliens in a Strange Land* (Waco: Word Books, 1973).
2. Ibid., p. 79.
3. Ibid., p. 82.
4. Ibid., p. 84.
5. Ibid., pp. 88–89.
6. Ibid., p. 94.
7. John Howard Yoder, *The Politics of Jesus* (Grand Rapids: Eerdmans, 1972).

2

Our Competitive Society

The annual dinner of the Touchdown Club is being held in the grand ballroom of the Sheraton Center, New York City. About five hundred athletes and football fans have gathered to hear speeches from notables, and to honor a young high school athlete who will receive the club's annual scholarship award.

Before the meal begins the chaplain from one of our service academies is called upon for the invocation. He approaches the microphone in splendid uniform and bows his head:

> Oh you, who threw out that first forward pass into the universe and called it earth, may we always remember that it is more important to be on your winning side than it is to win without you. Let us huddle with you daily, get your plays for our lives, move the ball in accordance with your will, and put it across the goal line for your sake. To you, our quarterback and coach, we give thanks for this event and the food we are about to receive. Amen.

There is no doubt that we live in a competitive society. And perhaps there is no place on earth where competition is as pervasive as it is in North America.

Sports

Competitive sports, both amateur and professional, are a major part of our American culture. From the time our children learn to walk and run, they are introduced to all kinds of competitive sports—baseball, football, soccer, basketball, hockey, swimming, gymnastics, track, golf, and racquet sports. They are suited up in uniforms as young as age five and, while some are burned out by age fourteen, others look forward to a lifetime career of competition.

The obsession with sports and winning wasn't always as strong as it is today. When I was a boy, the kids organized their own sandlot baseball games. We'd play "one-a-cat" or "scrub" and, on occasion, chose sides for a real game. The two best players became team captains, and players were selected on an alternating basis. We wanted to make the sides as *even* as possible. The rules were modified according to local conditions: in the garden was "out," and one base was allowed on an overthrow. The game might be more or less than nine innings; it didn't matter. If a new player showed up while the game was in progress, he or she (girls weren't excluded until the adults took over) was put on the side which would most tend to balance the game. A good player was assigned to the losing team, and a weak player was given to the winning team as a handicap.

Sandlot football, street-corner basketball, and backyard volley-ball—all operated in the same manner. The rules were relaxed, the equipment was whatever was available, and, believe it or not, kids had fun. You did not have any contact with organized sports until you got into junior high school, at about age twelve, and even then only a small percent of the kids were involved.

It's surely not that way now. Estimates say that ten to twenty million of today's children between the ages of five and fourteen are involved in adult-supervised competitive sports. Little League baseball claims to have over ten thousand leagues operating in more than thirty countries. There's Pop Warner football and Biddy basketball. In some school districts, the high school athletic programs are so well organized that an effective "farm system" reaches down into the elementary grades where kids are trained in basic plays to be used in later years. Harried parents spend hours behind the wheel of a car getting their kids to Little League games. And we hear of families who schedule their vacation plans around the dates when their children will be in sports camps.

What has happened to our society that we have organized our kids so tightly in competitive sports? *They* didn't ask for it! It was the adults who decided. Why?

The way in which we've pushed our kids into competitive sports isn't all that is new. Something else has blossomed as well—spectator sports.

Spectator Sports

Thanks especially to television, spectator sports have become a fantastic business. Millions of people across our country are glued to the tube week after week as they follow the seasons of the year: baseball, soccer, golf, tennis, football, basketball, and hockey. Interspersed with the seasonal sports are TV specials on swimming, track and field, boxing, gymnastics, wrestling, skiing, skating, weight lifting, bowling, auto racing, horse racing—the list goes on and on. The major networks compete fiercely to book important bowl games and the choicest of all sporting events—the Olympics. Their aggressiveness pays off because advertisers fork over huge sums of money to get their products in front of the millions of potential customers who have become addicted to spectator sports.

There were sports spectators long before television, but not anywhere close in volume to today's spectators. Years ago, perhaps you followed the local high school football or basketball team. Perhaps you sat on a park bench once or twice a summer watching the city recreation league in action. Maybe every now and then you'd make the trip to Yankee Stadium or Shibe Park or Wrigley Field to see the "big leaguers" play. But never before in our history has such a large segment of our population been involved in spectator sports to one degree or another.

One might conclude that television has merely moved the spectators from the ball park to the living room, but that's not true either. The expanded baseball, football, basketball, and hockey leagues are drawing a much higher turnout of spectators than they did twenty-five years ago. The fans love it!

Such is the quantitative side of what has been happening in sports in America. But there is also a qualitative side to it.

Perhaps what has happened can best be summed up by comparing the well remembered quotations of two famous sports figures of their day. Knute Rockne, coach of the Fighting Irish of Notre Dame back in the 1930s, said, "Try hard to win. But if you can't, be a good loser." A quarter of a century later, Vince Lombardi, the highly successful coach of the Green Bay Packers, occupied center stage as one of America's sports heroes. He summed it all up this way: "Winning is not the most important thing; it's *everything!*" Can you imagine Vince Lombardi saying, "Try hard to win"? Can you imagine him even *thinking* about advice for a loser?

Not only are we obsessed with winning, we are obsessed with being "number one." Time after time, we see the spectacle of sports fans jumping up and down in excitement with index fingers extended upward, shouting "We're number one!" Pittsburgh pops its cork when the Steelers come up with a Super Bowl win. Philadelphia throws a two-day party when the Flyers come home with the Stanley Cup. An entire state will come alive with excitement as their universities work their way up in the newspaper polls of the "top ten" in college football. UCLA, Michigan, Alabama, Nebraska, Georgia, Texas, Ohio State, Mississippi, Penn State—all of them share their glory or defeat with millions of fans in their state. But glory is there only if you're "number one."

During the decade of the 60s, the New York Giants had the best overall won-lost record in the National Football League. For five straight years, from 1965 through 1969, they finished in second place. Yet despite the fact that the Giants obviously had many winning seasons, they became known as the "born losers" simply because they never won the league title.

The Dallas Cowboys, on the other hand, actually *did* win division championships from 1966 through 1970. But because they either lost in the playoffs or in the Super Bowl, they were tabbed as "the team that couldn't win the big ones."

Reflecting upon his career in sports, Terry Bradshaw, star quarterback of the Pittsburgh Steelers, has frequently commented on the escalation of the need to be "number one." "It used to be," he said, "that you felt good about having a winning season. But that isn't enough anymore. It isn't even good enough if you win the league title. You've got to win in the Super Bowl, and the quarterback who loses that game is made to feel like a bum." Things have certainly changed since those days when Knute Rockne advised his players to "be a good loser!"

The pressure to be number one takes its toll in a thousand ways. Little League batters are screamed at by irate adults. Promising young swimmers are nagged at by their parents to practice more. High school records are falsified to grant playing eligibility to star athletes. Bribes and gifts are offered to promising high school football players to get them to come to a certain college, in spite of so-called codes of ethics. With a degree of regularity, our service academies dismiss large parts of their teams for cheating in class. And on national television, a prominent college coach, Woody Hayes, punches an opposing player in the face.

I have read studies which suggest that participation in competitive sports, especially contact sports, makes people more aggressive in all aspects of their lives. Other studies indicate that it is simply that naturally aggressive people find their way into competitive sports. It is also difficult to assess the effect of watching competitive sports. Some claim that through vicarious participation in competition, people are able to release aggressive tensions. Other studies suggest that watching contact sports increases aggression. It is obvious, however, that actions such as yelling, booing, jumping up and down, and cheering, which are normally not acceptable outside a sports arena, are legitimized inside it.

In varying degrees, then, competitive sports have been dominating the lives of more and more people in our country. Admittedly, some type of physical activity is important for all of us. But the question is: At what point do sports stop serving us and start possessing us?

Business

If sports is the most obvious example of American competitiveness, surely business can be rated second. American business and industry are nurtured by a competitive society. Notwithstanding a certain amount of rhetoric to the contrary, most Americans still believe that Adam Smith was right: if the economic system is permitted to operate freely, all of society will benefit. Although government has increasingly intervened in the free operation of American business, there is still ample evidence that competition is alive and well.

Perhaps no industry had been more closely identified with American culture than the automobile industry, whose ability to develop new engineering and styling that caught the fancy of buyers was immediately rewarded in the marketplace. In the cauldron of this competitive market, such classic names as Packard, Studebaker, DeSoto, Willys, and Nash have disappeared in the last twenty years. At the time of this writing, the huge Chrysler Corporation is hanging on only with the help of federally supported loans. Ford's American operation has lost money, as have both the domestic and overseas plants of General Motors. Who were the successful competitors? The answer is the foreign auto producers, who flooded the American market with the kind of car many people wanted to buy. A key factor, of course, was the soaring price of gasoline. The Japanese and Europeans, with their smaller cars, moved into the United States and were able to capture as much as one-third of new car purchases. The effect of this on employment in the American automotive and allied industries was devastating.

The American steel industry, in which I spent thirty-two years of my life, is also at a crossroads. The huge, fully integrated mills are no longer cost competitive with the newer, more efficient plants in Japan. In those products which require less costly equipment to produce, such as carbon bars, rods, and light structural shapes, the newer, smaller, regional mini-mills have captured most of the business. A number of circumstances have contributed to the current plight of the American steel industry—illegal "dumping" of foreign steel, inadequate generation of capital due to years of de facto federal price controls, environmental control regulations (which, while necessary, required large expenditures of money in relatively short periods of time), and a rather complacent attitude of management during the 1950s. The net effect has been the closing of older, unprofitable plants and a strong effort to operate more efficiently. Although jobs have been lost and careers cut short, the general feeling prevails that, in the long run, a freely operating competitive economy will be best for all of us.

Competition between airlines has been so ferocious in recent years that it is surprising some of the companies have survived as long as they have. Similarly, our daily newspapers include page after page of ads purchased by department stores, food chains, and discount houses, all competing to attract the customer to their location. Hotels, restaurants, resorts—all compete for the consumer's dollar. Buyers' guides are available to assist the consumer in finding the best places to eat or sleep, and to give prospective buyers the benefit of tests made on all types of consumer goods. All this in the name of competition. Banks, once the very model of cautious conservatism, have suddenly gone wild with all types of offers designed to attract depositors—high interest certificates, NOW accounts, IRAs, special services, and gifts.

There is even a segment of the business community which exists simply because people want to be successful competitors in business. The shelves of bookstores and libraries are filled with books which reveal the secrets of being a successful salesman, motivator, manager, or investor—you name it. Magazines and trade journals are filled with similar types of articles. Not too long ago I came across a magazine called *Success Unlimited,* with the subtitle "The Magazine with a Positive Mental Attitude." Recently my mail contained a "sensational offer" of a home education course on "The Psychology of Winning." Billed as a course "for winners who want to put it all together," the program offered a book and twelve cassette tapes for "only $49.95."

A popular trend in religious books in recent years has dealt with the power of positive thinking and "how you can be what God wants you to be." The TV preachers on Sunday morning frequently present a success-oriented theology, which certainly has appeal to businesspeople.

As in sports, business competition spawns undesirable and illegal activities. In an effort to reduce costs, product quality may be compromised. Sometimes the consumer is hurt. In an effort to increase output, unsafe work practices may be overlooked. Sometimes the workers are hurt. In an effort to increase volume of sales, dishonest advertising or deceptive packaging may be resorted to. Sometimes the customers are cheated. In an effort to ease the competitive pressures, illegal price fixing or bribes may be tried. In an effort to keep abreast of competition, industrial espionage may be undertaken. For all of these abuses, society, operating through the system of laws, has to set the rules of the game.

Even when operating fully within the rules, competition in business can be rough, destructive, and all-consuming. In a *Time* magazine article (June 16, 1958), Charles Revson, founder of Revlon, Inc., reflected much of America's image of the competitive business when he said, "I don't meet competition; I *crush* it!"

In his book *The Gamesman,*[1] Michael MacCoby suggests that competing just for the joy of winning seems stronger now than at any other time in American business. He recalls that a generation ago high value was placed on loyalty and obedience to the company.[2] It was the generation of *The Organization Man,*[2] when one's duty was to fit in with, conform to, and support the company totally. MacCoby says that today, to be on a winning team is more important than security or even pay. High achievers in business today get their kicks from being part of a winning organization.

Critics of American business and industry frequently say, with some cynicism, that free competition is an illusion. They postulate that the power interests in this country are so strong that they can control the economy while pretending that it is operating freely. The antibusiness activists claim that a few hundred powerful men in our nation totally control the economy, and that what is really needed is a dismantling of all large businesses so that the little people can have a say in economic decision making. I feel the evidence does not support such a position. The mass of Americans are daily making economic decisions which do affect major corporations. Who buys the Toyotas and Volkswagons, the Korean shirts, the shoes from Hong Kong, the television sets from Japan? Ask the managements of A&P, Sears, Roebuck & Company, and General Foods who makes the economic decisions which affect their futures.

We certainly do not have a totally free and unbridled economic system, nor should we. But it is clear that competition is the engine which drives the system we do have. There is no doubt that competition in business and industry has been for the welfare of many, many people. The question is, however, is competition working for us, or are we working for it?

The Educational System

Perhaps the earliest point at which a child encounters a competitive institution is when he or she begins school. No matter if there is a grading system or a pass-fail philosophy, the child quickly learns that he or she is performing alongside others who may be better or worse. And the farther the child advances in school, the more pronounced becomes the competition. There are IQ tests in the early years, and SAT tests later. Honor rolls, deans' lists, magnet schools, special education, and class rankings are all part of the environment as the child moves through the educational system. National Merit Scholarship exams and competitive college scholarship exams pit students against each other.

In the 1965–75 era, when a flood of young people were trying to get into college and space was scarce, entrance requirements were very demanding. Many universities would not consider an applicant who was not in the top third of the high school class. During this period, we lived on the Main Line of Philadelphia in a rather affluent school district. Conestoga High School had established a history of having about eighty-five percent of its graduating seniors go on to college.

Most of the parents naturally expected to send their sons and daughters to college; and not just *any* old college, either. They had in mind the most prestigious universities. But panic set in when these high-demand colleges insisted upon considering only those in the upper one-third of the class, How can eighty-five percent of the class be in the upper third? Obviously, the pressure was on the kids and the competition became acute. As might be expected, there were numerous instances of cheating in exams, and an underground network developed to sell theme papers written by college students.

The June 10, 1980 issue of the *Wall Street Journal* carried an essay by Gerald F. Seib entitled "Why Are They Cheating?" By interviewing both students and faculty, Seib concluded that cheating at college is significant and increasing. He cited cases of stealing forthcoming exams from administration offices, paying to have someone else take your exam, purchasing theme papers, and using hand calculators to cheat in class. One of the students who admitted to cheating said, "I think people would be much happier to see an A on their report card by cheating than a B they got by studying a lot."

The article continues with an explanation of how "students rationalize their cheating by citing such pressures as grade inflation, overcrowded campuses, intensified competition for graduate degrees, and the presence of professional cheating mills." The competition for graduate school is especially intense in the medical field. Michael Hooker, associate dean at Johns Hopkins University, is quoted as saying, "The undergraduate world is perceived by many students as a Darwinian jungle where they are competing with each other." The essay concludes with a summary remark by "Gary," a student who steals exams. He explained that today's students are "basically . . . reward oriented."

So competition is alive and well among the students of America. But it isn't only the students in the educational system who are the victims of competition. Teachers, faculty, and administrators have been swept along by these forces as well.

When enrollments in our schools and colleges decrease, a corresponding reduction in teaching staff must also occur. Whether union contract provisions control or whether the administration has a free hand, the scramble goes on to survive staff cutbacks. In an effort to reduce the number of tenured positions, colleges frequently release teachers prior to the time of tenure in what can only be considered a ruthless exploitation of people. Consequently, many faculties today are engaged in vicious power struggles for control of jobs, departments, and the school itself.

A young professor friend discussed the competitive pressures he has experienced within the academic community. He had somehow assumed that once he got a teaching job at a decent college, his status problems would be behind him. "Pressures to compete continue at all phases of my professional life," he admits. "It seems like you never arrive. With each achievement, I found new challenges facing me which I could not ignore. There is always the more prestigious position ahead of me; there is always the more prestigious school to which I could be invited. Getting articles published is not enough; they have to be in the right journals. There is pressure to secure research grants to continue my work, and there is pressure to earn tenure."

When people are under pressure, some of them crack, and some of them cheat. A friend, who was chairman of a science department at a well-known college, has estimated that about fifty percent of all scientific theses and postdoctoral research today is fraudulent!

Educational institutions compete among themselves. Every metropolitan area has its so-called best school district and best high school. Colleges and universities are constantly trying to achieve superior ratings and reputations. Within any academic discipline, there are certain schools which are recognized as being tops in their fields. Naturally, the pressure is upon administrators and faculty to maintain such reputations. In the years when I was at Lehigh University, the football team was not doing too well, but we easily compensated by convincing ourselves and the community that the Lehigh Marching Band was the best in the East.

I am not trying to build a case that all competition is bad for our educational system. When used properly, it can be the means of encouraging excellence. It can be a positive force. Bertrand Russell once said, "I do not think that ordinary human beings can be happy without competition, for competition has been, ever since the origin of man, the spur to most serious activities." Competition is a means for helping to develop one's full potential, in education as in sports. What must constantly be checked, however, is the manner and degree to which we compete, and the effect that it has on people. In short, does competition in the field of education serve us, or are we slaves to it?

The Arts

Can anyone in our American culture really escape the pressures of competition? Is there any area into which it has not crept?

Some of my nieces and nephews have gone into the fields of fine arts and the performing arts to avoid the "rat race." But the "rat race" was there, too, awaiting them. Unless one has an outside source of income, economic realities have to be faced, no matter how simple the life style may be. Either the art must provide some income, or else an outside job must be taken to support the creative efforts.

Apart from the financial considerations, rare indeed is the artist who can paint without recognition. To have one's work noted by an article in a newspaper or journal, to win an award in an art show, or to be asked to exhibit or perform somewhere is the kind of psychic encouragement needed by all creative people. And, after all, who wouldn't prefer first prize in an exhibit over second or third?

In developing their careers, young actors and actresses need to amass as long a list of credits as possible. Once you're on the way, the siren sounds of success become more clear. Broadway has its annual Tony Award as well as the New York Critics Award. Who wouldn't want to be part of a cast that is so recognized? Hollywood has its annual Oscar Awards for the best picture, best actor, best actress, best director, best photography—best, best, best. To win an "Oscar" has been the dream of thousands in the film industry. They have been "possessed" with the desire.

Weekly Nielsen ratings tell us which television shows are drawing the largest audiences. New series which show up poorly in the ratings are quickly dropped. Every moment of TV time is competing to attract the attention of the viewers. Not even the newscasters can escape. In the early days of television, news was simply and factually presented. Today, it must be entertainment, and the newscasters of the major networks compete fiercely to win the public's attention. Even the two-minute weather forecast must be presented in the most entertaining way possible.

While newspapers and magazines compete with each other for high circulation numbers, they also compete for annual awards for best news coverage, best editorial, best feature article, best news photo, and so on. Again, the pressure to achieve recognition can cause aspiring newspaper writers to lose integrity. In 1981, the well-respected *Washington Post* had to return a Pulitzer Prize for distinguished journalism when it was discovered that the aspiring young writer had completely fabricated her story.

Awards are offered for architectural excellence, for photography, for dance, for sculpture, for musical competition. Indeed, there is no part of the creative or performing arts in which there is not some form of competition.

Religion

Not even religion has escaped the success syndrome. The basic measure of success for local congregations or national denominations has been membership growth and the level of financial giving. Too often, the "best" clergy are those who can "pack 'em in" on Sunday morning, "keep 'em happy," and balance the budget. Controversy, the addressing of social issues from the pulpit, and prophetic preachings are to be avoided, because if people are unhappy with the pastor, they'll go elsewhere. The competition will gladly take them in.

In recent years, I have had many occasions to work closely with the regional and national offices of three major Christian denominations in the United States. It has been a sad revelation to observe the sometimes sharp competitiveness which exists in departments of the same denomination and among the professional staff. The national offices of our Christian churches are no more exempt from competition for attention, power, and career advancement than are our business corporations.

The past few years have seen a fantastic growth of the so-called "electronic churches." Along with this has come a competitiveness that pays off in huge sums of money. National Religious Broadcasters, Inc., in their 1978 report, claimed over eight hundred and fifty stations and program producers as members, and more than five hundred million dollars of *purchased* radio and TV time in a year.

The air time purchased does pay back handsomely. Estimated gross revenues in 1978 among the big hitters in this field were: Oral Roberts, sixty million dollars; Garner Ted Armstrong, sixty-five million dollars; Pat Robertson and his "700 Club," thirty million dollars;

Jim Bakker and his "PTL Club," twenty-five million dollars; Rex Humbard, eighteen million dollars; and that fast-rising superstar, Jerry Falwell, thirty-two and one-half million dollars. With the rising power of the Moral Majority, it is certain that 1981 incomes are well above the 1978 totals just cited.

Not only are these electronic preachers slick fund raisers in a highly competitive field, but they invariably press a "success oriented" style of the gospel. One way or another, the message seems to come through: "Praise the Lord and send the money, and you will be blessed in your life."

Another interesting phenomenon is the marriage of sports and religion as found in a number of so-called Christian Sports Ministries. I have had some contact with the granddaddy of the sport/faith group—the Fellowship of Christian Athletes. To an outside observer, the leadership of FCA is having a real identity struggle. Initially favoring an "evangelical outreach" and "winning souls for Jesus" within the sports world, FCA has recently moved in the direction of dealing with how the Christian faith does relate to competition and the abuses of it. I believe the Fellowship of Christian Athletes can do us all a favor if they work hard at this issue. It is needed. Less concerned about the issues of faith and competition are Pro Athlete Outreach, based in Phoenix, Arizona, and Athletes in Action, an arm of Campus Crusade for Christ, with headquarters in San Bernardino, California. These two groups seem to operate on the philosophy that since most people are attracted to winners, the ideal way to evangelize is to promote a gospel of "success." I have trouble with that.

Get Yourself a Blue Ribbon

It was Henry Clay who said, "Of all human powers operating in the affairs of mankind, none is greater than that of competition." He was speaking of business competition, but if he were alive today, I'm sure he'd widen his range a bit.

For years we've had the Miss America contest. More recently, we've had a Miss World, Miss Universe, Mrs. America, Mr. America, and who knows what others. In most instances, these titles are won after a long series of local and state competitions. Various organizations have a Mother-of-the-Year award and a Dad-of-the-Year award. Communities will name their "citizen of the year" or "humanitarian of the year." Clubs and associations will name their "salesman-of-the-year" winners or "young president-of-the-year." The list boggles the mind.

There are "Who's Who" listings for all kinds of categories— volumes of them. *Harper's Bazaar* annually selects seven women achievers who are chosen "for their willingness to beat the odds."

We still have county fairs with awards for best apples, best corn, best poultry, best pigs, best apple pie—you name it. If you don't have a blue ribbon for something, it's because you just haven't tried. Out there somewhere there's a blue ribbon or an award or a first place awaiting you. Just go out and get it!

Perhaps this chapter is guilty of overkill. But the point needs to be made strongly that all of us are part of a competitive society. Competition is one of the "powers" with which Christians must deal. It is my conviction that in the past twenty-five years, this power has become more intense and pervasive in American society. Millions of our people are so obsessed with the need to be "number one" in sports or business or entertainment or whatever that they are literally driven by it. The power has possessed them in a demonic way.

Even for those who are not driven by the desire to be first, there has been a general acceptance of a value system which measures the worth of a person by how well he or she has performed. It is a value system directly contrary to the gospel of Jesus Christ.

NOTES—CHAPTER 2

1. Michael MacCoby, *The Gamesman* (New York: Simon and Shuster, 1976).

2. William H. White, Jr., *The Organization Man* (New York: Simon and Shuster, 1956).

3

The Dark Side of Competition

As we sat down to dinner, our oldest daughter, Shelley, made an announcement. "I've been nominated for vice-president of the junior class."

"Hey, that's great, Shelley!" we responded. "When will the election be held?"

"In two weeks," she replied, "but I'm not too sure what I should do."

"What do you mean? What's the problem?" we asked.

"Well, in the next two weeks, all of the candidates will be running campaigns. It's kind of like local political campaigns. You know, posters, speeches, and that kind of stuff," she explained.

"So?" we asked. "Don't you plan to do the same?"

"I feel funny about it," she said. "You see, the girl I'm running against is black. She really wants to win, and I know it would mean a lot to her and other black kids in the school."

The time was the mid-1960s. The Civil Rights movement had begun to change in the direction of "black pride" and a "black is beautiful" emphasis. Our family was very much aware of the shift since we had been involved with the race issue for a number of years. Shelley's instinct was on target. For a largely white high school class to elect a black girl to office would be a real boost for blacks in our community.

Shelley continued, "I honestly don't care that much about being elected. I think if I were running against a white kid, I probably wouldn't do much campaigning. But because Sue is black, it makes it harder to decide. If I don't try hard, it will look like I'm a do-gooder trying to help out a poor black girl. And I think she'd be angry if it appeared that I 'gave' her the win. But if I really try to win, I very well

could beat her, and it just isn't as important to me as I know it is to her.
What a mess!''

The competitive society presents us with dilemmas galore. There is
no doubt that the forces of competition have helped people to achieve
excellence in many fields of endeavor. And it is utter foolishness for
anyone to think that we can opt out of our competitive culture. But it
is important that we be alert to the dangers of competition. Knowing
them, we may be able to make good judgments as to how we handle
this strong force.

There are three factors which need to be considered by Christians
in the competitive society: the effect of competition upon others, the
effect upon oneself, and the matter of self-identity.

Effect Upon Others

In many types of competition, there are clear winners and losers.
Most sporting events conclude with the determination of a winner.
Likewise, contests such as spelling bees, beauty pageants, political
campaigns, horse shows, and the like will identify who is the winner.
If the event pits one person against another, as in a chess game, or one
team against another, as in football, the conclusion also clearly iden-
tifies the loser. When a field of contestants is competing, such as in a
race, those who did not win are less likely to be distinguished as losers
unless, of course, one happens to be in the very last place.

Other forms of competition do not clearly identify winners but, in
more relative terms, deal with such matters as leadership. The business leader of today may not be in first place next year. Without a
fixed end point for the competition, there can be no final, declared
winner or loser. Poor Nielsen ratings for NBC this year can be
different next year and, as long as the contest continues, who is to say
who is the ultimate ''winner''?

Finally, there is that type of competition which has virtually no
effect on others. If I press myself to jog two miles in less time or to
read a book a week or improve my swimming, the achieving of such a
goal has no impact on anyone else.

It is clear, then, that different types of competition have vastly
differing kinds of effects on others. One kind of competition we need
to be mindful of is that in which our winning causes another person to
lose.

The term "being a good loser" did not come into being just by accident. It can hurt to lose, to fail, to feel inferior. If I am able to control or ignore the feelings of defeat, I'm a good loser.

But what about those who are unable to overcome those feelings of failure or defeat? What about people who have a poor self-image? What happens when they lose? When the stakes are high and the preparation has been intense, the hurt which comes with losing can be devastating. Adlai Stevenson, for example, a man of remarkable self-control, said of his presidential loss to Dwight Eisenhower, "It hurts too much to laugh, and I'm too old to cry."

Just because we are able to handle defeat does not mean everyone else can do the same. Just because we may not have a great need to win, it does not follow that others feel likewise. We need to recognize that for some people, it is very important to win, and the sting of defeat can be debilitating.

Some who make a case for participating in win/lose contests argue that the experience of losing is helpful in Christian growth. Writing in *The Christian Century* (October 10, 1979) on "Theologizing in a Win/Lose Culture," Carnegie Samuel Calian cited some of the chief benefits connected with losing. Losing, he said, is a necessary part of living. "Losing can be valuable because it reminds us of our finitude" —it "gives us an opportunity to reexamine our goals and opportunities." Calian also noted that, "Losing can remind us that our life is in need of some redemption." Moreover, "We can learn from our failings something of the profundity of Christ's cross." In short, "losing puts us in touch with our humanity."

Now really! Can you imagine trying to convey these arguments to a twelve-year-old Little Leaguer who struck out every time at bat for five straight games? Even for an adult, the logic can come around on itself. Let's get out there and lose; it's so good for us. And if it's good for us, it's good for our opponent. So if we love him more than ourselves, we'll humiliate him in tennis because the losing experience will be so good for him. Charge!

Some people react to the use of the term "winners/losers." They feel that we should always be working to help people be winners. Situations should be designed so that instead of a win/lose outcome, there can be only win/win outcomes. There is some validity to this viewpoint. For example, the best negotiations between two parties are effected when both sides feel they have won important objectives. Furthermore, if we can help people develop a good enough self-image, the losing of a contest should not result in the lowering of self-esteem. In that sense, although the contest itself may have had a winner and a loser, in fact, neither party was a "loser."

But having said all that, we cannot deny that there are people in our culture who do see themselves as losers and for whom another losing event can be destructive. Are there some ways in which we can ease the severity of losing in bipartisan contests? Those sports which lend themselves to handicapping work in this direction. Golf is one sport where the handicap approach works well. To the extent that the handicapping system works in golf, two opponents start off on the first tee, exactly equal, although they may be of significantly different ability. Whoever wins usually does so by a narrow margin, perhaps the final putt on the eighteenth green. The loser is not humiliated by the superior player.

Professional sports endeavor to keep their teams roughly equal in talent by means of a draft system in which the weaker teams get early picks of the high potential college players. This handicap system does not produce the equivalency found in golf, but it is true that on any given day, almost any team in the National or the American Football Leagues can beat almost any other team. Of course, this type of handicapping is not done for the sake of the players, but for good commercial reasons. The more evenly the teams are matched the better the games will be, resulting in the attraction of more fans. But there are not too many sports which lend themselves to the handicapping approach.

Recognizing that a mature adult should be able to handle a losing situation better than a youngster, should we perhaps turn our attention toward lessening win/lose situations among the young? Some people think we should. Gary Warner, former director of communications for the Fellowship of Christian Athletes, has written an engaging book on sports titled *Competition*.[1] He sees enough harm in win/lose contests among young people that he strongly advocates the following points: "no contact sports before age fourteen (ninth grade), and in non-contact sports, no more than the keeping of league standings—no playoffs, no all-star teams, no post-season banquets, no off-season training, and no media coverage of youth sports games before ninth grade, except for the printing of scores.'' Warner's concern is that youth sports spawn philosophies that stay with the individual throughout a lifetime.

Should the Christian refuse to participate in a win/lose competitive situation? That's a difficult question to answer. On the one hand, it seems to be an extreme way of insuring that we are not party to the beating down of another person or group. Frankly, I enjoy win/lose contests. I enjoy watching football on television and would miss not seeing the annual Super Bowl. On the other hand, there is obviously some point beyond which win/lose competition can be harmful. The intensity and extent of win/lose sporting events certainly has increased in recent years. The question is, have we gone too far? If so, how do we de-escalate?

If the win/lose type of competition can have devastating effects on the other person, is the type of competition which has no fixed end point less destructive? It would seem that as long as the contest continues, there is always the chance for the loser to reverse the situation. In fact, however, the open-ended type of competition can also be very destructive.

For ten years, I was a sales manager for a major steel company. My responsibility dealt with steel for the construction industry. We had a large number of steel mills and fabricating shops which depended upon our sales department to keep them working. I felt a very strong responsibility to the workers in our plants. The welfare of their families was affected by how good a job we did in securing orders. The nature of steel buying for construction is such that you cannot create more of a market; it is limited by other factors. In other words, people would not go out and decide to build more bridges or buildings because we decided to lower our prices or sent around more sales-people. Construction activity responds to other influences such as interest rates, capital expansion, population changes—all beyond our control. Therefore, at any given time, there was just a limited market for steel purchased for construction. This meant that to the extent our sales force was successful, our competitors were not. The more we got, the less there was for our competitors. In very slow years, if we did well, perhaps some lights would go off in Pittsburgh or Gary or

Los Angeles. I certainly saw that I had a responsibility to the workers in our plants. But did I also have a responsibility to the workers in our competitors' plants?

It strikes me as interesting that while the church has given very little thought to the role of the Christian in a competitive society, our federal government has deemed the effects of unbridled competition to be potentially harmful enough to have created a whole body of law relating to behavior. Both the Federal Trade Commission and the Department of Justice diligently monitor the actions of American business to insure that there is compliance with our antitrust laws. The primary focus of these laws is on those who stand to be hurt by the competitive system. It is presumed that if one company is so large it monopolizes a market, the American public will be hurt for lack of competitively priced products, and potential competitors will be hurt for lack of resources to compete with the one giant. It is also presumed that if competing companies are permitted to work in concert with each other, the public will be hurt because they may have to pay fixed prices or have limited choices of products or producers. These laws create an interesting situation where, on the one hand, it is illegal to be so friendly with your competitors as to agree upon prices or markets or other such factors; on the other hand, it is also illegal to be so hostile to your competitors that you intentionally try to drive them out of business.

Since the antitrust laws of most other industrial nations are not as tightly drawn, one wonders from whence came the concern about the evils of competition which caused these laws to be drafted. Was there a Christian perspective which played a part, or was it purely secular?

What about open-ended competition in the classroom? What happens to a child in a system which continually rates him or her as inferior to others? How many years are needed to convince a human being that he or she will always be mediocre, or even a failure? How many of God's creatures are living a life far below their potential because of a school rating system which conditions them to be at the bottom of the pile?

Moreover, if we work for a large company or other organization, there is competition for advancement. The higher one goes in the pyramid of organizations, the fewer become the openings for promotion. Some make it; some do not. For those who have invested heavily in their career, the failure to win a coveted promotion can be devastating. It can, in some cases, signify the end of the line for that person.

The self-employed of a community compete with each other for clients. If the supply of dentists exceeds the demand of the community, some will succeed in business while others will not. Every year in our country there are thousands of failures of small businesses. In many cases, these failures represent the loss of the total assets of a family. Everything is gone.

So whether it is in the win/lose type of competition or in open-ended competition, those who lose or fail can be badly hurt.

Effect on Oneself

At its worst, competition may cause us to let go of our own sense of values and decency. Who will ever forget that startling moment when Woody Hayes, that highly respected coach of Ohio State and an idol of many sports lovers, slugged a young football player from another college in full view of millions of television viewers?

Hockey is one of the most violent of contact sports. Can you imagine any hockey player attacking people on the street the way he attacks opponents on the ice, and getting away with it? But in the Philadelphia Spectrum, the so-called bullies of the NHL, the Flyers, are given license to commit mayhem upon all visiting teams to the cheers of adoring fans. What does that kind of violence do to the person who lives with it every day? Can it be parked in the locker room along with the skates?

Gary Warner, whom I mentioned earlier in this chapter, tells about how one of his coaches tried to teach him to "hate" his opponent. Warner was instructed to humiliate his opponent in an athletic contest before the opponent had a chance to embarrass him, and all of this under the label of "competition." But do we really want our youngsters to participate in a system that uses hate as a coaching technique for "psyching up" the players?

It is not certain that brutality in sports or in any other form of competition carries over into the rest of one's life. But we do know that hatred can. One who is taught to hate the opponent can find hatred spilling over into other areas and relationships. Competition can indeed spawn brutality and hatred.

The pressure of competition can also generate dishonesty in sports.

Records are falsified to prove eligibility, money passes hands illegally, and some players learn how to break the rules of the game without being caught.

In June of 1981, a former University of New Mexico basketball coach was convicted of over twenty counts of fraud and making false public vouchers. Commenting on the case, District Judge Phillip Baiamonte said, "Naturally rules and laws were broken. Is anyone really surprised? This is a problem that probably exists at every major college and university in the country."[2] Competition can yield dishonesty.

Greed is another fruit of the competitive system. How much is enough? Is it enough to have a winning season, or must the team win the division title? Shouldn't league champions get post-season bowl opportunities? Who wants to come out of a bowl game second best?

Is it enough to run a business that merely stays in the black? Shouldn't there be constant growth in size and profitability? Why not strive to have the most profitable company in town or in your industry?

How many people covet the job of their supervisor? And, once having attained that job, there is always the next one waiting. What's wrong with wanting to be at the top of the organization? How much do we really need in life? If the competitive system offers us more than we really need, shouldn't we reach out for it? What's wrong with having more than you need?

In *The Christian Athlete* magazine (November–December 1980) Ross Fichtner, former college all-star and later pro player for the Cleveland Browns and assistant coach for the Chicago Bears, wrote about greed in professional sports. He took aim at such things as excessive salaries, faking injuries, and reneging on contracts. Fichtner complained that greed had reached down into high school and youth league ranks because coaches wanted to compile good records. "No matter what they say," he wrote, "coaches with this approach are out to improve their record and advance up the ladder, not build character. I say let kids enjoy their high school playing days for all they're worth."

A technique used by many coaches to get maximum effort from their players is to appeal to pride. It is considered a virtue for an athlete to take pride in his or her ability and team. On the one hand, a sense of pride can improve a poor image one may have of oneself. On the other hand, it can very easily spill over into arrogant egotism where one truly believes "I am the greatest!" When does pride become arrogance?

If I am the greatest, then where does God stand? If I am a self-made person, then where does the creator fit in? If I owe my success to my skill and perseverance, then what do I owe to God?

Competition, however, should not be viewed in a totally negative way. Competitive activities can develop excellence, self-confidence, and leadership. The virtues of competition are regularly paraded before us so that they need no further advocacy here. Yet, what is often overlooked, are the dangers of competition—how it can hurt those who compete. If competition has the power to develop violence, hatred, dishonesty, greed, and pride (arrogance) in those who engage in it, then it indeed does have a dangerous side to it. Competition must therefore be handled with care. As Seneca once wrote, "The better man may win, but he will be the worse for his victory."[3] Indeed competition can be dangerous!

Self-Identity

We need to be aware of the effect that our competing has upon others. We need to be alert to what competition can do to ourselves. But there is another aspect of competition which is even more serious. It has to do with self-identity.

As Christians, we take the theological position that God has initiated a relationship with us. He is our Creator; we are God's children. Our baptism was the point at which God came to each of us personally and, without any merit on our part, stamped us as his own and assured us of his love and acceptance. Nothing we as humans have done or could ever do can earn this relationship with our Creator.

Christians are identified relationally. "I am a child of God." We pray to "our father." Jesus spoke of "his children." All others are our "brothers and sisters."

In the competitive society, identity is based on what we do, not who we are. The more we are involved in competition, the more our identity is shaped by what we do, and our worth is based on how well we do. But our worth in God's eyes has nothing to do with being successful or unsuccessful in competition.

Based on his record, Terry Bradshaw, a star quarterback, is

"worth" more in football than some rookie quarterback with a last-place team. A two-time "Oscar" winner is "worth" more in the film industry than an extra, simply on the basis of past performance. Someone in the top third of a high school class is "worth" more to a college admissions director than someone in the bottom third. So what does all this business of worth do to our understanding of our relationship with God?

Ask some Christians if they believe they will get to heaven, and the reply frequently is, "I hope so. I try to do my best." Where did the idea originate that God's acceptance of us is based on how well we have done? No doubt it comes out of our competitive society. A chief danger in the competitive society, therefore, is the way in which its measurements of worth becloud and ultimately destroy our understanding of the grace of God.

Competition in the Kingdom

I have read material claiming that Jesus was a terrific competitor, that he fished for mens' souls, competed with the devil in the wilderness, contended with the money changers in the temple, and debated with the religious leaders of his time. Jesus is pictured as a proud winner.

Rubbish.

In Matthew 20, the mother of James and John asked Jesus to give orders that in his kingdom, her sons would sit at his right and left hand. This request angered the other ten disciples. But Jesus quieted them by pointing out that "whoever would be great among you must be your servant, and whoever would be first among you must be your slave."

The three synoptic Gospels also tell the story of how the disciples argued about which of them was the greatest. Jesus told them about a little child and then concluded, "For he who is least among you all is the one who is great" (Luke 9:48). That hardly sounds like a competitive person speaking.

Jesus lived and moved in a competitive society just as we do. But he was not hooked by the powers of competition. He did not *need* to compete.

As Christians, we confess a belief in life after death. How we picture that life after death varies among us. But ask yourself this:

Does your vision of the afterlife, "heaven," or whatever you may call it, include Little League games and the Super Bowl? Will there be managers and workers? Will some live in big houses and drive fancy cars while others live in shacks? Will some wear medals and others not? Will there be grades and awards and prizes for the best citizens?

My vision of the afterlife includes none of these things. And if I cannot believe the kingdom of heaven will have all the trappings of our competitive society, what does that have to say about my relation to competition in the here and now?

Christians are in a society in which the superhuman power of competition prevails. We cannot escape it. We must live with it, but we must also learn how not to be dominated and enslaved by it. We do need to ask some questions. In a society ruled by the power of competition, to what degree do Christians participate? Where do we draw the line for ourselves and our children? Is competition affecting our society in undesirable ways? If so, do we boycott parts of it, or try to change it?

For evangelical Christians, there is also a very large question: How do we communicate to others the fact of God's love freely given without any merit in a culture which constantly barrages us with a philosophy that merit is the only fair way of receiving anything? How do we help people see that their identity in life is based on whose they are, not on what they do?

Competition can draw people toward violence, hatred, greed, dishonesty, and arrogant pride. The gospel gives people the freedom to love and to be peaceful, satisfied with enough, generous toward others, and modest. Competition is a power that can enslave people. The gospel is a power that can free people.

NOTES—CHAPTER 3

1. Gary Warner, *Competition* (Elgin, Ill.: David C. Cook, 1979).
2. *Allentown* (Pa.) *Sunday Call-Chronicle* (July 12, 1981).
3. *Epistolae* XIV.

PART TWO

THE WITNESS OF THE BIBLE

4

A Theology for a Competitive Society?

What does the Christian faith have to say about our competitive society? What are the biblical and theological perspectives which address this powerful force in our culture? Does competition advance the kingdom of God or frustrate it? Is competition, like money, a neutral thing whose morality depends on how people use it? Does our understanding of stewardship conflict with our understanding of servanthood in the realm of competitive activities? In what way should Christians relate to this culture of competition? In short, is there a Christian theology for a competitive society?

For several years, I have been in search of such a theology. I have found virtually no books or essays in which theologians specifically address the issue of a competitive society. In meetings or gab sessions with clergy friends, I have been throwing out the question of a theology of competition for a number of years. Generally, there is a long pause in the conversation. It is as if I had asked a question which had never occurred to anyone. Perhaps it hasn't. Perhaps competition is so basic to our culture that we have not considered asking about its theological implications. William Stringfellow reminds us that "Human beings do not readily recognize their victim status in relation to the principalities."[1] Do we perhaps not see that we are frequently victims of the force of competition?

From time to time, I am asked to be a conference leader for clergy. The assigned theme usually concerns the ministry of the laity. During question-and-answer sessions, however, the clergy try to find out how I have related my faith to my job as manager in a large corporation. From the way questions are phrased, I can usually identify those clergy who find it difficult to believe one can be both a Christian and a

45

corporate manager. When that kind of questioning begins to flow, I use the opportunity to share some of the dilemmas I have faced, many of which relate to competition. I'll freely admit to the pervasiveness of competition in my job, my country, and even my church. Then I'll ask the big question: "Pastors, where can a lay person like me go to get some perspectives on competition from a Christian theological viewpoint?"

Silence. There is almost always silence.

Then I'll ask them if, just for fun, I can play the role of a lay theologian and throw out some possibilities. They always agree.

Starting with the Old Testament, I point out that there is a constant theme that the Israelites, God's chosen people, will ultimately prevail over all their enemies. As a matter of fact, Yahweh is identified as a God who will bring victory to his people without their help. As one reads the Exodus account, it is clear that the Israelites did nothing to bring about the defeat of the Egyptians. Yahweh did it all. I remind my audience of Moses' words when the Israelites, out of fear of the Egyptians, said they would rather be slaves than die in the wilderness. "Fear not," Moses answered. "Stand firm and see the salvation of the Lord, which he will work for you today; for the Egyptians whom you see today, you shall never see again. The Lord will fight for you, and you have only to be still" (Exod. 14:13–14).

Joshua's win at Jericho (Joshua 6) and Gideon's defeat of the Midianites (Judges 7) were most certainly not due to the superiority of the Israelites. It was Yahweh's intervention that brought victory. Moreover, there are several instances recounted in 2 Chronicles where the people lost when they depended on their own strength and won when they relied upon God. The prophet Zechariah said, "Not by might, nor by power, but by my Spirit, says the Lord of hosts" (Zech. 4:6).

I tell the pastors that from all this I conclude that God's chosen people were not to be contesting for their needs. Rather, they were to put their complete trust in the Lord who would provide for them, even to the extent of defeating their enemies. Victory there would be, but not by the hands of the people. "Therefore," I explain, "I see the Old Testament as the testament of God leading his people into the 'winners' circle' without any effort on their part."

In the New Testament, the sermons and parables of Jesus again suggest that God's people are not to be anxious about their needs. God will provide. In fact, those who do concentrate on overproviding for themselves, as did the wealthy landowner, are suprised to find it has all been for naught (see Luke 12:16–21).

But there is another theme in the New Testament—the servant theme. "If anyone would be first, he must be last of all and servant of all" (Mark 9:35). "For every one who exalts himself will be humbled, and he who humbles himself will be exalted" (Luke 14:11). The consistent theme in Jesus' sayings is that we should *not* strive to be first, but rather seek to serve others.

Looking at the life of Jesus himself, of course, one could conclude that he was a born loser. He was born in a cow barn and died on a cross between two thieves on the garbage dump outside the city's walls. In the eyes of the world, that's hardly being "number one"!

Christians are quick to point out that in the resurrection Christ was proclaimed the ultimate and total victor. He was victor over death itself. But if we are to pattern our lives after the life of Jesus, then it seems clear that we are not only to avoid competing with each other, but we must place ourselves in a postition below others so that we can serve them.

Summing this up for the clergy, I say, "I think the New Testament is the testament of the losers. The theology of the cross calls us to be servants to people even to the point of losing our lives. Moreover, since there is no evidence in the Old Testament that God's people are to be contending for anything, and since the New Testament lifts up the image of the suffering servant, one must conclude that there is no biblical basis for Christians to be involved in competition.

That statement usually achieves the desired result of bringing out a number of rebuttals. Frequently, the pastors will speak of using our talents to the best of our abilities, and occasionally one will refer to Genesis 1 with its admonitions to "have dominion" and "subdue the earth." And I will concede that my home-made theology may be all wet. "But," I add, "if my theology on competition based on biblical texts is wrong, please give me a better one."

Again, silence. No replies.

Inevitably, after the program, some clergy approach me individually to give me their thinking. Frequently they will begin, "I didn't want to say anything in front of the rest of the group, but . . ." (This must be a competitive group, I think.) Their positions run full range. Some will say that the Christian faith is indeed a theology of the cross, that we are to serve others unto our own death, and, therefore, that a Christian must avoid all forms of competition. At the other extreme, some clergy will say that God gave talents to use, and that we should use them to the very best of our ability for the glory of God. One pastor even said, "It's the American Way!" By far the largest group will confess that there are no easy answers, that too little thinking has been given to the subject, and that it depends upon the circumstance as to what will be the Christian stance.

I wish I were as certain of the biblical perspectives on competition as I pretend to be in front of the clergy. In all honesty, I do not have a clear understanding of the role of the Christian in a competitive society. The Bible can be used to support arguments on either side of the issue. There is, for example, a rather constant thread running through the Bible that might be called "responsible stewardship." We are cocreators with God, and we are to treat the gifts of his creation responsibly. We are to use our God-given talents in service to others and to the glory of God. That suggests to me that in a competitive society, we use our talents for the greatest good we can. If that means competing in education or sports or business or whatever, so be it. If that means accepting a role of leadership in government or business or various organizations, then that is the way we must go. To refuse to use our God-given talents in matters involving the well-being of our brothers and sisters would be "irresponsible stewardship," in my opinion.

And yet there is that undeniable thread through the New Testament of the last being first, of the meek inheriting the earth. The image of the leader as servant is present in both the Old and New Testaments. Jesus' harsh criticism of the religious leaders of his time, his many warnings about being wealthy, and his numerous references to being a servant are disquieting notes for one who competes in our world as a "responsible steward."

Two of the parables of Christ seem almost contradictory in their application to a theology of competition. They are the parable of the talents and the parable of the laborers in the vineyard.

In the parable of the talents, a master gives each of three stewards a talent to use while he goes on a trip. One steward is able to multiply the talent tenfold. The second steward shows the returning master five talents. The third steward returns but the one talent to the master because he was afraid he would be punished if he lost it. The master was angry with the third steward, so he gave his one talent to the steward who had ten and banished the nonproducer. Jesus concludes the parable by saying, "For to every one who has will more be given —but from him who has not, even what he has will be taken away" (Matt. 25:29).

That is a nice, capitalistic-type parable. To the best investor belong the rewards. For most of us, the story is simply a statement of the way things work in our society.

But then, there is that other troubling parable about the laborers in the vineyard. The master hires some workers for an agreed upon wage early in the morning. He hires some others at noon. Finally, a few are put to work only an hour before quitting time. When it comes time to pay the workers, the master does it in reverse order, starting with those who came last. He paid the last the same amount he had promised the workers who started at noon. When he got to those who had worked all day, he paid them the same amount as the others. Naturally, they complained about the injustice of it all, since they had worked all day in the blazing sun. The owner turned to them and said, in effect: "My friends, I am not being unfair to you. You agreed on the usual wage for the day, did you not? Take your pay and go home. I chose to pay the last man the same as you. Surely I am free to do what I like with my own money. Why be jealous because I am kind?" Jesus concludes the story with the words, "So the last will be first, and the first last" (Matt. 20:16). Can you imagine either management or labor agreeing to that type of contract?

At first glance, the parable of the talents seems to be just, while the parable of the workers in the vineyard seems to be unjust. However, when both stories are examined in the light of God's gift of grace to us, they reverse positions. When we remember that God's gift to us is based on a relationship and not on how long or how hard we have worked, then the parable of the laborers in the vineyard makes sense. But in that same understanding of God's gift of grace, what is the meaning of the parable of the talents? Isn't this essentially a works-righteous parable?

If we move on to an examination of Paul, I do believe there is evidence that he was a fairly strong competitor. At the time of his conversion, he was determined to stamp out the followers of Jesus because he was a strict Jew. Paul certainly had his differences of opinion with Peter and the other early Christians in Jerusalem, but his dogged perseverance prevailed. He was determined to spread the Word and many times risked life and limb to do so. He was indeed a very gutsy person. And he was not above reminding people of all the things he had done for his Lord.

Paul frequently uses competitive imagery in his letters. In 1 Corinthians he writes: "Do you not know that in a race all the runners compete, but only one receives the prize? So run that you may obtain it. Every athlete exercises self-control in all things. They do it to receive a perishable wreath, but we an imperishable. Well, I do not run aimlessly, I do not box as one beating the air; but I pommel my body and subdue it, lest after preaching to others I myself should be disqualified" (1 Cor. 9:24–27). In his Letter to the Galatians, Paul talks about making sure . . . "lest somehow I should be running or had run in vain" (Gal. 2:2).

Paul also liked to talk about armor, which certainly is used in competing with others. He wrote of the "armor of light" (Rom. 13:12), the "armor of righteousness" (2 Cor. 6:7), and the "whole armor of God" (Eph. 6:11). In the Letter to the Ephesians, he elaborates to the extent of identifying the pieces of armor: the belt of truth, the coat of mail of integrity, the shoes of the gospel of peace, the shield of faith, the helmet of salvation, and the sword of the words which come from God.

What does all this mean? Are we to conclude that Jesus did not compete, while Paul did? And, if so, are we to pattern our lives after Jesus or Paul, or doesn't it really matter? Are these Bible texts germane to our present situation or are they not?

I confess that I have not been able to satisfy myself that there is a biblical position for or against competition per se. As in so many other issues, proof texts can be found to support almost any argument. I have been told that some European theologians have written on the subject. Their writings apparently have not come to the attention of those American theologians with whom I have talked, and they certainly have not come to the attention of American laity.

I am not alone in this frustration. Robert K. Greenleaf, former

Director of Management Research at American Telephone and Telegraph Company, has done much thinking and writing on the subject of Christian servanthood in today's culture. In one of his recent books[2] he tells of attending a conference entitled "The Judeo-Christian Ethic and the Modern Business Corporation." Greenleaf reports, "There were about twenty-five theologians of the major faiths present. In the papers and the discussions there was frequent reference to 'unfair' competition, but I do not recall a single question by a theologian about competition per se."

It is Greenleaf's opinion that somehow competition must be "muted" in our society. He says, "If theologians will not lead this move (and I sense no initiative from this quarter), practicing servants will, and theologians will rationalize after the fact."

Is Greenleaf too much of a pessimist? Is it possible for our theologians to work with the laity in opening up new studies on how our timeless beliefs relate to the present realities of a technological, industrialized, competitive society? Is it really too much to ask that here in America some serious theological attention be given to this modern driving power that touches the lives of all of us and, in some cases, crushes some people and possesses others?

NOTES—CHAPTER 4

1. William Stringfellow, *An Ethic for Christians and Other Aliens in a Strange Land* (Waco: Word Books, 1973).

2. Robert K. Greenleaf, *Servant: Retrospect and Prospect* (Peterborough, N.H.: Windy Row Press, 1980).

5

Biblical Images for Monday

Just as the Bible does not provide definitive instructions for dealing with competition, it also does not give us recipes for handling the principalities and powers of our society. Contrary to what some Christians claim, the Bible does not give Americans "God's position" on such issues as equal rights for women, prayer in the schools, or SALT treaties.

But the Bible does contain basic truths and some fundamental principles which can be applied to our contemporary problems. There are several images, which are biblically based, that may provide direction in dealing with our modern-day "principalities and powers."

In But Not Of

In John 15:19, Jesus says to his disciples, "If you were of the world, the world would love its own; but because you are not of the world, but I chose you out of the world, therefore the world hates you." If this verse were to stand by itself, one would conclude that the followers of Christ are to disassociate themselves from all worldly activities. In the past two thousand years, many sincere Christians have followed exactly that path.

However, in John 17:18, Jesus prays for his disciples, "As thou didst send me into the world, so I have sent them into the world." Standing by itself, this verse suggests that the followers of Christ are to be totally immersed in the affairs of the world. The verse appears to contradict the "out of the world" statement of John 15.

The apparent contradiction is resolved by John 17:16. The Revised Standard Version of the Bible treats it this way: "They are not of the

world, even as I am not of the world." The Jerusalem Bible and the
Good News Bible translate it, "They do not belong to the world any
more than I belong to the world." Jesus is saying that his followers are
to be actively involved in the world without being owned by it. The
first part of this verse defines the arena of discipleship, while the
second part defines the accountability of discipleship. The followers
of the way do not "belong" to the world; they belong to the Lord and
are accountable to him. We are to be in the world but not of the world.

Strangers and Sojourners

The New English Version of the Bible translates John 17:16 as
"They are strangers in the world, as I am." We define stranger as one
who is a newcomer. The stranger is not known by many people. After
some time in the new location, the stranger starts to know people and
is known by them. He or she gradually ceases to be a stranger.

But the word stranger in the Old Testament was understood a bit
differently. A stranger was simply one who was not a Jew. The person
could be well known to the community and could be a functioning part
of it, but because he or she was not a Jew, the stranger never really
"belonged."

In like manner, when the Jews were living among other people,
they saw themselves as "strangers and sojourners." The word
sojourner is frequently coupled with or used in place of stranger in the
Old Testament.

In Gen. 21:34, we read how Abraham sojourned many days in the
land of the Philistines. When Sarah died in Hebron, Abraham went to
the Hittites to ask for some property for a burial place. He said to
them, "I am a stranger and a sojourner among you; give me property
among you for a burying place, that I may bury my dead out of my
sight" (Gen. 23:4). During their captivity in Egypt, the Israelites
considered themselves sojourners for 430 years (Exod. 12:40). The
Levitical laws specified how the Jews were to treat strangers and
sojourners (Lev. 16:29; 18:26; 25:6, 47).

Exodus 12 contains instructions for the Passover meal. The rule
was that no sojourner or hired servant should eat of it (12:43). Before a
stranger could partake of the meal, all the males in the family had first
to be circumcised—that is, become Jews. In short, unless one became
a Jew, one would always be considered a stranger and sojourner.

The word "alien" is also used by some translations in place of stranger. This word can provide additional insight.

We have sponsored a number of different refugee groups over the years. There were East Germans, Cubans, Ugandans, and Vietnamese. It was always a joy to help them become acclimated to their new home as fast as possible. Some settled in faster than others, but their desire was to be "taken for Americans" when they mingled in a crowd. But no matter how well they adjusted, they were officially "aliens," not Americans. No matter how much they looked like Americans or talked like them, they were legally aliens until that day when they renounced their former citizenship and pledged their allegiance to the United States.

In the same way that the Jews looked upon others as strangers and sojourners, they also understood that in a sense they, too, were sojourners upon the earth. For example, in giving the laws to Moses, the Lord decreed (Lev. 25:23) that the land should not be sold into perpetuity, "for the land is mine; for you are strangers and sojourners with me." The New English Bible uses the words "aliens and settlers." The psalmist echoes this understanding when he sings (Ps. 39:12), "Hear my prayer, O Lord, and give ear to my cry; hold not thy peace at my tears! For I am thy passing guest, a sojourner, like all my fathers." This imagery suggests that, as God's people, we dwell in the world as sojourners or aliens, being fully a part of it but always knowing our allegiance lies elsewhere—with God. Beyond this is the understanding that the physical world is God's and we are here as his guests.

We are, indeed, strangers and sojourners or, if you will, aliens in a strange land.

Captivity and Freedom

The Biblical imagery of "principalities and powers" carries with it the implication of captivity. The principalities and powers seek to dominate or hold captive those who come under their influence.

If there is one theme which carries through the Bible from beginning to end, it is the message that God delivers his people from captivity. The history of the Jewish nation, as it unfolds in the Old Testament, recounts a series of instances in which God, in his mercy, brings his people from captivity to freedom. The Exodus from Egypt is the best-known example. In all cases, the freedom was the result of

God's loving action, not the result of any meritorious deeds by which the Jews could demand that God give them their freedom.

And, of course, the gift of freedom is at the heart of the gospel. The life and death of Jesus Christ was and is the means through which God proclaims his gift of freedom for us. Paul said it well in the closing verses of Romans 8: "For I am sure that neither death, nor life, nor angels, nor principalities, nor things present, nor things to come, nor powers, nor height, nor depth, nor anything else in all creation, will be able to separate us from the Love of God in Christ Jesus our Lord" (8:38–39).

As a young monk, Martin Luther struggled hard over the issue of how to earn the love and acceptance of God. No matter what he did for God, he was never convinced that he had done enough to merit God's acceptance. At that critical moment in his life when Paul's words in Rom. 3:24 "they are justified by his grace as a gift" finally sank in, Luther became a free man. He was liberated from a captivity of believing that his acceptability before God was based on what *he did*.

Our understanding of the liberating message of the gospel is constantly being assaulted by the principalities and powers, especially in this competitive society. In a culture in which our identity is determined by what we do and our worth is based on how well we do it, how difficult it is to keep in mind that fantastic news of the gospel that our identity is really based on whose we are, and our worth is fully assured simply as a free gift of our Creator.

That gospel assurance is absolutely crucial if one is to be able to function in today's society. When we deal with worldly problems that are so complex that there are no clear solutions, we need to know that, having done our best, we are still assured of God's love and acceptance no matter what the outcome. As we deal with those dilemmas wherein someone will get hurt no matter what we do, we need to know that, having given the situation the best consideration we possibly could, we must make a decision. As Luther said, we "sin boldly," knowing that regardless of what happens, our forgiveness is assured.

God does not call us to be successful; he calls us to be faithful.

It is my belief that so many people are unable to look forward to their Monday world simply because they do not sufficiently know or understand or believe the gospel. It is nothing less than a scandal that the Christian church today has been unable to bring the liberating reality of the gospel into the lives of its people.

Priests

The final image which is needed to function in the Monday world is that of a priest. If we understand that we are in but not of the world, if we see that we are but sojourners in a strange land, and if we know that by God's grace alone we are acceptable, then what is our role? The psalmist asks the same poignant question in another way: "How shall we sing the Lord's song in a foreign land?" (Ps. 137:4). The answer is: Our role ("singing the Lord's song") is to be priests—all of us.

One of the unfortunate ways in which the principality of the church institution has been able to imprison us has been through the distortion of our understanding of priesthood. Most Christians today understand a priest as an ordained religious leader who has certain privileges and duties within the religious organization. This concept is much too narrow and is not supported biblically.

By definition, a priest is a mediator between God and the people. The priest represents God to the people and represents the people to God. It is through the priest that the Word and love of God come to the people. It is through the priest that the prayers and intercessions for the people are presented to God. The Reformation leaders dusted off the biblical understanding of priesthood by proclaiming that all of the followers of Christ had a calling to be priests to one another. Luther said, "Every baptized Christian is a priest already."[1] Luther meant *everybody,* women as well as men.

Exodus 19 describes Israel at Mount Sinai following the deliverance from Egypt. God instructs Moses: "Thus you shall say to the house of Jacob, and tell the people of Israel: You have seen what I did to the Egyptians, and how I bore you on eagles' wings and brought you to myself. Now therefore, if you will obey my voice and keep my covenant, you shall be my own possession among all peoples; for all the earth is mine, and you shall be to me a kingdom of priests and a holy nation" (Exod. 19:3–6). Those words were addressed to all the Israelites, not just to the religious leaders.

Regarding the promise of a new Jerusalem, the prophet declares (Isa. 61:6): "You shall be called the priests of the Lord, men shall speak of you as the ministers of our God." The reference again is to all the people of the new Jerusalem.

In the First Letter of Peter, referred to as "the calling of a Christian," the thread of God's people being a "holy priesthood" continues. "But you are a chosen race, a royal priesthood, a holy nation, God's own people, that you may declare the wonderful deeds of him who called you out of darkness into his marvelous light" (1 Pet. 2:9). The reference to God's people as "priests" appears several times also in the Book of Revelation. The salutation of the letter says, "To him who loves us and has freed us from our sins by his blood and made us a kingdom, priests to his God and Father, to him be glory and dominion for ever and ever. Amen" (Rev. 1:5–6). In all these references, it is all the people of God, not just the religious leaders, who are called to a priestly role.

As contemporary priests, we bring before God the needs and cares of people through intercessory prayer. We bring to God the joys and thanks of people through worship and thanksgiving.

As contemporary priests, we bring before the people God's Word and his love. Through what we say and do, through the style of life which is ours, we witness to others of the liberating nature of the gospel. Through our calls for justice in society, we fulfill the prophetic nature of being a priest. And through our acts of feeding, housing, clothing, working among, healing, and visiting people, we are being the channels of God's love in society.

The idea of calling oneself a priest is so foreign to most Christian laity that they frequently reject it as if it were blasphemy. Some feel that to convey the mantle of priesthood to all believers is to reduce the power and authority of those who have been called to the office of priest in one of our denominations. However, the universality of the priesthood does not diminish its power; it multiplies it.

Moreover, most laity are convinced that the arena of the priest is in the church doing religious things. And if the priest does venture beyond the walls of the church, it is to say and do religious things.

Karl Hertz, in his fine little book, *Everyman a Priest,*[2] has this to say about such a narrow limitation upon Christian priesthood:

> Worship as an independent activity of the religious person, separated in kind and in meaning from his daily existence, is a travesty of divine action. In fact, those who worship in this manner are polytheists, paying

homage to one god on Sunday and other gods on weekdays. . . . To say
that dimensions of life exist in which I cannot act as a priest is to deny
that these dimensions are under the sovereignty of God. Yet that is
exactly what we do time and again—when, for example, we think that the
religiously concerned layman ought to become a minister or when we
think that the proper technique for "getting into industry" is to hold
prayer meetings in factories rather than to solve the difficult problems of
labor-management relationships.[2]

I am convinced that if contemporary Christians can see themselves
as being in the world and not of it, as being strangers and sojourners,
as being liberated by the gospel from all principalities and powers, and
as being called into a priestly role in the world, the "Monday blues"
will disappear. To be sure, we will still "thank God, it's Friday!" but
we will also be able to approach Monday with a freedom and sense of
purpose which we have never known before.

We need next to look at a few more of the contemporary principalities and powers which seek to dominate our lives.

NOTES—CHAPTER 5

1. Ewald M. Plass, ed., *What Luther Says,* vol. 3 (St. Louis: Concordia
Publishing House, 1959), pp. 1, 139.
2. Karl H. Hertz, *Everyman a Priest* (Philadelphia: Fortress Press, 1960).

PART THREE

PRINCIPALITIES AND POWERS

6

Occupation

The television screen is blank. Suddenly, the buzz of an alarm clock is heard. A bed lamp goes on and a hand reaches over to shut off the alarm. As the man sits up in bed, a solemn voice on the television intones, "The day cannot begin soon enough for a man possessed by a single aim in life. He is compelled by his drive to win." That drive, it turns out in the commercial, is to be on the winning team of stockbrokers. If you want to make good investments, you should call your Bache broker and join that winning team.

"A man possessed by a single aim in life?"

In 1963, Harold Gray, while a vice-president of Litton Industries, was in a serious motorcycle accident. His one leg was broken in seventeen places, his hip was shattered, and for six weeks the doctors did not know if they could save his leg. Yet Gray missed only two days of work. He immediately converted his hospital room into an office by having his files and secretary transferred to his bedside. Gray continued to manage his business while flat on his back.

In anticipation of his retirement as Chairman and Chief Executive Officer of General Motors, Thomas A. Murphy reflected upon his career. Without trying to be overly modest, Murphy observed that he never really ran the company. Instead, he suggested, the company largely ran him. He added, however, that he felt it was important for every individual "at some point" to have control over his or her life.

Our occupation is one of the principalities which constantly seek to dominate our lives. It is true that some of us are literally "possessed" by our jobs. It should not be concluded that work in itself is evil simply because it can dominate us. On the contrary, work is a basic need for the fulfillment of human life.

The creation stories in Genesis tell of God's plan for humans to do work. The Mosaic laws contained many rules relating to work. Jesus' parables frequently dealt with work and workers.

The Apocryphal Book of Ecclesiasticus, one of the wisdom books, has much to say about work. For example, it has this to say about craftsmen:

> All these rely upon their hands,
>   and each is skillful in his own work.
> Without them a city cannot be established,
>   and men can neither sojourn nor live there.
> Yet they are not sought out for the council of the people,
>   nor do they attain eminence in the public assembly.
> They do not sit in the judge's seat,
>   nor do they understand the sentence of judgment;
> they cannot expound discipline or judgment,
>   and they are not found using proverbs.
> But they keep stable the fabric of the world,
>   and their prayer is in the practice of their trade.
> (Ecclus. 38:31–34)

The need and right to have a job is becoming so universally accepted that Peter Drucker in a *Wall Street Journal* article (March 4, 1980) suggested that we are on the verge of treating jobs as a type of property rather than a type of contractual claim. Before the industrial revolution, land was the true "means of production." Ownership of land, therefore, gave people access to economic rewards including social standing and political power. Today, Drucker points out, the "means of production" for the vast majority of us is through our job, usually with some organization. The job is now the means of access to economic benefits, social status, and power.

Most of the developed noncommunist countries have been moving more and more toward insuring employees certain rights which have precedence over outside creditors and legal owners. For example, Japan now guarantees lifetime employment (for men) in many government and business occupations. In Europe, a system of "redundancy payments" prevails under which, should an employee be laid off, he or she will receive compensation equivalent to full salary for the remainder of the employee's lifetime. The High Court of the European Community recently ruled that "redundancy payments" must even survive the employer's bankruptcy.

In the United States, we are moving in a similar direction. For example, employee pension claims take precedence over all other claims against a bankrupt company, up to thirty percent of the net worth of that organization. Some states have enacted laws which prescribe the obligation an employer has to the workers in the event of plant closings or movements.

Our society recognizes the right of owning "real property" such as land, of owning "personal property" such as money and possessions, and of owning "intangible property" such as copyrights and patents. "It is not too farfetched," says Drucker, "to speak of the emergence of a fourth—the property in the job—closely analogous to property in the land in pre-modern times."

The need and the right to work, therefore, are basics of our society. From a religious, social, economic, and political standpoint, work is good. Simply because it is good and necessary, however, does not mean it is not without danger for us. Our occupation, our job, our work has the potential, the *power,* if you will, to enslave us. We can become victims of our occupations, prisoners of our jobs.

Our occupation, whether that of physician, homemaker, businessman, or craftsman, demands certain things of us. These demands are virtually open-ended—limitless—if we permit them to be. They represent obligations to our work, but unless we are alert to the demonic potential of our job, the demands run uncontrolled, and we are thereby enslaved. It is important to recognize the kinds of demands which can ultimately dominate us.

The Demand of Time

Quite obviously, every occupation demands a certain amount of our time. In some types of work, the commitment is rather rigidly set; the plant shift starts at 8:00 A.M. and ends at 4:00 P.M. But in many occupations, the worker can devote as much time as he or she wishes. Doctors can set their own hours, as can tavern keepers, housewives, repairmen, and artists.

Some time ago, a *Wall Street Journal* article (August 20, 1980) noted that "chief executives typically work sixty to seventy hours a week, travel six to ten days a month and give up many of their weekends." Reporting on a survey jointly done by the *Wall Street Journal* and the Gallup Organization, the article stated, "The heads of the 1,300 largest U.S. corporations accept as necessary the rigorous work routines. Most believe success in their careers demands that they make personal sacrifices, and most put their jobs ahead of their families and themselves."

We have a name for such people: *workaholics*. The excessive dedication of time to one's work is not limited to the owners or managers of our institutions. Anyone can sign up as a workaholic.

In one of our district sales offices, Bill had a clerical job which normally could be handled adequately between the hours of 8:00 A.M. and 5:00 P.M. But he was always at his desk at 7:15 A.M. and was still hard at work at 5:30 P.M. He frequently cut his lunch hours short because he was "too busy." For a period of time, I observed his work, thinking that possibly we had unevenly distributed the assignments among his group. But I discovered that Bill's workload was on a par with the others. He was not slower than they were, nor less intelligent. He just somehow had a knack of manufacturing more work for himself to do. For a while, I spent some time with him in an effort to show him how he could get all his work done just as well in less time. But it gradually dawned on me that Bill *wanted* to work longer than the others. He wasn't trying to impress his superiors; he just seemed to have a need to work longer hours. He was a workaholic.

For some reason, the caring and helping professions seem to attract or produce (whichever comes first) fine workaholics. Nurses, doctors, social workers, clergy, and lawyers commit massive amounts of time to their work. Some of these people truly can say, "Thank God, it's Monday!" because they are so taken up in their work. Nevertheless, they are as hooked by the craving for work as the alcoholic is by the compulsion to drink.

Apart from those who may have deep psychological needs, the fact remains that the nature of our work can become so engrossing that we increasingly commit more and more time to it until it has become our master. We become one-dimensional people.

My grandfather spent all of his working life as an employee of the local post office. Through the years, he worked his way up to being the postmaster in Allentown. Every day of his life he was at the post office at 6:30 A.M. and did not return home until 6:00 P.M. His job was his life. He had absolutely no other interests. He never missed a day's work in fifty years of service. The time finally came when he had to retire and, although he had always been in perfect health, he was dead within six months. He had nothing to live for when the job was gone.

It is sad to travel through Florida or Hilton Head Island or other places where the "successful" go to retire. So many of them seem empty, unhappy. They read the morning paper, play golf, have cocktails, go to dinner, go to bed—day after day. This is the retirement legacy for those who committed all their time to their work.

Our jobs *can* dominate our lives by capturing all our time.

The Demand for Energy

It is such a common occurrence that it has become a stereotype. Mother comes home from her job, walks into the house, and is asked a simple question by "Junior." She explodes in anger. Father comes home from work, plops down in a chair, reads the newspaper, and speaks to no one. The next-door neighbor gets out of his car, walks up the driveway, and as his dog comes to greet him, he gives it a kick.

It used to be that we said these people had a "hard day at work." In recent years, we have developed a technical term for the more extreme cases. We call it "job burnout."

Besides the demand of time which our occupations place on us, they also demand a commitment of energy. Depending upon the nature of the job, the energy demands may be excessively high. We call such jobs "stressful."

The air traffic controllers at our major airports do not work long hours. But during the time they are on duty, they must be constantly attentive to what they are doing. One slip, one slight error, one overlooked blip on the radar screen may result in the loss of hundreds of lives. The stakes are so high that the controllers must give their job their total energy. The stress connected with being an air traffic controller is so great that few can stay in the position for many years.

Job burnout has been most frequently observed in the healing and service professions such as medicine, social service, and law. Especially vulnerable are nurses, surgeons, divorce and criminal lawyers, police officers, teachers, and the staffs of mental hospitals and hospices.

Our daughter, Buffy, is a psychiatric nurse who works with teenagers in two major hospitals. She says that the needs of her patients are limitless: "They will take everything out of you and still need more." Being aware of the severe emotional drain, Buffy and her associates try to measure out their energy expenditure so as not to become totally drained.

Job burnout can occur in almost any job, however. If for some reason the job can hook the worker in such a way as to command total attention and energy, burnout can occur.

In recent years, the subject of job burnout has received attention in a number of business-related publications. The April 23, 1981 issue of the *Wall Street Journal* featured a page-one article on burnout among corporate managers and what was being done to treat the problem. In the article, Herbert Freudenberger, a New York psychologist who claims credit for the term, defines burnout as "a depletion of energy."

In an earlier article in the same newspaper (November 11, 1980), Christina Maslach, associate professor of psychology at the University of California at Berkeley, described the three stages of job burnout. "First," she said, "there is emotional exhaustion, a feeling of being drained, used up, of having nothing more to give. Secondly, there is cynicism, a callous insensitive regard for people, a don't-knock-yourself-out-anymore-for-others attitude." The final step, she explained, is the burntout person's belief that he or she has been unsuccessful and that all job effort has been fruitless.

Both *Wall Street Journal* articles describe a similar approach to treatment. First, it is necessary to look at the job itself. If it can be reconstructed to reduce energy drain, that is the way to go. Reconstruction may involve major changes in job descriptions and responsibilities. Or it may involve simply keeping a record of specific things to avoid which produce unusually high energy drains. For example, the interaction with one specific person may generate stress that is out of proportion to other relationships in the working environment. If the functional relationship to that one person can be removed, the problem may ease significantly.

If the job cannot be reconstructed, then ways must be found to interrupt the constant drain. In some cases, getting the individuals to do something strictly for themselves, on a routine basis, may ease the energy drain. Going off the job site to have a cup of coffee with a friend or having lunch at a variety of locations are examples of some trivial steps which may help.

Burntout workers are urged to get into some new activities which will energize their lives. One executive, on the verge of total burnout, was rejuvenated through participation in a federal job-training program conducted by his company.

If the cure for burnout is to stop the energy drain, the prevention of it is to limit one's commitment of energy to one's job. Some jobs have a low risk of depleting one's resources, while others are much more dangerous. It is important to look at our jobs objectively and make certain we know to what extent they are depleting our energy.

The principalities of occupation can capture and destroy us by draining all our energy.

The Demand for Loyalty

Among his hierarchy of needs, Abraham Maslow lists the "need to belong"—a middle-range necessity which must be met after the needs of food, clothing, shelter, and security. All of us need to belong. One of the requirements of belonging to any organization is to make a commitment of loyalty to it. It is more than giving time or energy. Organizations to which we belong ask that we be supportive of them. Our families are a good example. While we may have arguments and differences within our families, before the rest of the world we will defend and be supportive of them. Our jobs ask the same of us.

The problem is, however, that because our jobs can be and sometimes are demonic, they are capable of accepting our total, undivided loyalty. When we offer exclusive loyalty to our jobs, we have proclaimed a new god in our life.

With the possible exception of our families, our commitments of loyalty tend to be in direct proportion to our commitments of time and energy. A person who is working and is also in a wide variety of civic organizations will naturally tend to divide loyalty among all his or her interests. But when we hear that chief executive officers of major corporations work sixty to seventy hours a week and travel six to ten days a month, the odds are high that heavy commitments of loyalty are involved.

The commitment of loyalty to one's family usually represents the last line of defense against total commitment to the job. Many a battle has been fought between a person's family and a person's job for the acknowledgment of who comes first.

In my thirty-two years in the business of marketing steel, I have

68THANK GOD, IT'S MONDAY!

seen many cases where families have suffered because decisions were made time and again to put the job first. Among my associates and our customers, there are many cases of broken marriages and alienated children. I know of dozens of marriages which continue as a shell of a relationship because the working member deserted his or her partner for a love affair with a job.

Six out of ten executives surveyed by the Gallup Organization (reported in the August 20, 1980 *Wall Street Journal*) said they felt personal sacrifices had to be made in order to succeed in a job. Eighty percent of that group confessed that their family lives had suffered because of their careers. Some spoke of failing to provide enough parental guidance and of feeling guilty about neglect. Others said they missed seeing their children grow up. A few said they felt they hardly knew their children. More than one in ten said serious family problems had resulted from their work situations.

The division of loyalty between job and family is especially difficult when there is a large company in a small town. When we moved from Detroit to our central office in Bethlehem, Pennsylvania in the late 1950s, it became apparent that the company influence was almost always present. There was never an overt effort to control the community; it was just that wherever you went—PTA meetings, shopping, cocktail parties, church, theater, or sporting events—Bethlehem Steel associates were there, and frequently we "talked shop." In a sense, the company was present wherever we went.

Ten years later, when we moved from Philadelphia back to Bethlehem, we made a deliberate effort to put distance between the job and the family. We built a home fifteen miles away in an area where there were no other Bethlehem Steel people. Some of my superiors interpreted this step as a sign of disloyalty. Actually, it was my way of insuring loyalty to my family. With a bit of distance between the job and the family, there were far fewer occasions for the company presence to be felt in our home.

There are some dark sides to the issue of job loyalty. Some people, out of their loyalty to their company, will become embroiled in immoral, unethical, or illegal actions. Many liability claims for defective products trace back not to a policy decision of management, but to a decision made by an employee at a lower level trying to do a better job for his company. In many manufacturing operations, there are product specifications that have built-in safety factors. So if a particular product run falls slightly under specification or perhaps varies slightly above and below within a certain lot, a plant superintendent may authorize shipment, knowing that the odds are heavily in his favor that the product will perform satisfactorily. The pressure to do so increases if he is paid on a bonus system based on the high percentage of products acceptable for shipment.

It is not unusual for an overzealous salesman to overstate the capabilities of his product. For example, if the customer wants an assurance that a product will perform in a certain way and the salesman knows from experience that it will in ninety-nine percent of the cases, does he give unqualified assurance or mention the one percent likelihood that the product might not perform? In an effort to increase production or to make up for lost time, will a plant foreman permit the workers to short-cut some safety procedures which he feels are redundant anyway? Will a salesman agree to fix prices or divide up a market with some of his competitors so that his company will do better, even though he gets no personal gain from such an action? Will a division head agree to establish a secret slush fund to be used for bribes and kickbacks in an industry or country where such practices are commonplace?

We read of such things happening all too frequently. In most cases, such illegal or unethical practices are absolutely contrary to written company policy and are done without the knowledge of top management. But because the employees have been so carried away with loyalty to the company, they do things they would never consider doing for themselves in their own private lives.

There are times, however, when top management knowingly does or authorizes something which is illegal. Then a different kind of loyalty problem arises down the line. Should the employee call the attention of appropriate authorities to the illegal action or, out of loyalty, should nothing be said? Should someone "blow the whistle"?

David W. Ewing, executive editor of the *Harvard Business Review* and author of several articles on corporate ethics, points out the difficulty of "whistle blowing." He says, "The old master-servant relationship that goes back to the code of Hammurabi still applies. That was the first code that defined a servant's obligation to the master—to be loyal."

Most frequently, when an employee does have the courage to turn the public spotlight on a top-management evil, he can forget about his career. A "promotion" may come through to an unacceptable location, or a redefinition of responsibility may strip him of anything significant to do, or he may even be found to have a health problem (often mental) and placed on sick leave. The demands of loyalty sometimes carry a very high price.

The principality of occupation demands time, energy, and loyalty from us. It will gladly accept our total commitment of all three, thereby claiming another captive. The degree to which we are able to control and measure our commitment of time, energy, and loyalty to our job is a measure of our freedom. Do we control our jobs, or do our jobs control us?

Some of the ways in which the principality of occupation can dominate our lives are fairly evident, but some are quite subtle.

The Influence of the Boss

In *The Oppressed Middle: Politics of Middle Management*,[1] Earl Shorris tells about the totalitarian tactics of Henry Ford. He says, "Ford was so certain of his own unique claim on the understanding of virtue that he sent company executives to the homes of his workers to determine whether they were living properly. Those whose standards of morality, cleanliness, child rearing, and so forth did not conform to Ford's were advised to change their ways or be dismissed."

Shorris points out that the principles of Calvinism gave the great entrepreneurs of the late nineteenth and early twentieth centuries leave to adopt the leader principle that their very success proved them to be the elect of God and men, and that therefore they had a mandate to make men over in their own image. Those days are gone, but the influence of the boss still continues in varying degrees.

For young, ambitious people just starting out in their careers, the supervisor can easily become a role model. If the boss happens to be a workaholic and commits all of his or her energy and loyalty to the company, the young followers are likely to be influenced. They think they see what is needed to advance in the company, and they may agree early in their careers to pay that price. Some young people have talked to me of their strategy for a high "up front" commitment to their job with the thought of easing off when they have reached a respectable position in the organization. That plan usually fails for several reasons. First, the so-called "respectable position" always seems to move higher on the organizational chart the higher one gets on the ladder. Ambitious people really are never satisfied. More importantly, once one's reputation has been established as a hard-working, extremely dedicated worker, it is very difficult to consciously ease up. A reputation is at stake. Finally, total commitment can become addictive. Like a junkie, once we're hooked it's very difficult to shake the habit.

Even if a worker does try to control the degree of commitment to the job, there will still be problems. The boss, who is at his or her desk an hour before starting time and an hour after quitting time, really is upset by people who arrive and leave on the appointed hours of work. Many times I have heard the comment, "He's *only* a 9 to 5'er" when the performance of a worker is being discussed. In short, workers can get negative performance evaluations for raises and promotions simply because the boss expects them to put in as many hours as he or she does.

In fact, some supervisors are so influenced by their observations of an employee's commitment of time, energy, and loyalty that they will promote an incompetent person just because he or she is highly dedicated. They measure the wrong factors.

The Pressure to Conform

Some occupations will tolerate individualism and a degree of non-conformity among the workers. I say "tolerate" because I believe it is basic to the nature of a demonic principality to try to control all the aspects of a person's life. But some fields of endeavor need creative people, and these people tend to resist conformity. In order for companies to attract and keep such people, a degree of freedom for the individual must be present. But most organizations pressure people to conform in a wide variety of ways. Many occupations have dress codes. I'm not talking about wearing uniforms as nurses or police officers; I'm talking about unwritten but universally accepted understandings of what should and should not be worn. Bankers have traditionally worn very conservative dark suits—always white shirts. Ties and shoes were conservative. In more recent years, in keeping with the changing image of banks, suits have become a bit less conservative, blue shirts are okay, and ties are a bit livelier. But that's it. You certainly don't want to do business with the vice-president of a bank who looks as if he just came from the race track.

Steel salesmen working for the major companies can dress a bit less conservatively than the bankers, but not too much. Steel salesmen working for the smaller mini-mills may wear sport coats and bright shirts and ties. More than one customer has made the statement to me that "all you big steel salesmen look alike."

In business circles, there are recommended colors for use in certain situations. If you're going to make a major presentation to your management or to an important client, go with dark blue or gray suits. We even have an expression of wearing a "sincere blue" suit. These colors convey authority and power. Brown is to be worn in passive situations where you want to convey support or receptivity. And never, I repeat, never, wear a green suit. Olive is the closest you may come. Wing-tip shoes are okay, and oxfords are, too. In recent years, loafers, if they are conservative, have won acceptance. Boots are out.

I got the message on dress code very early in my career, and not from any of my bosses. Soon after arriving in Detroit for my first sales assignment, I bought a very light blue summer-weight suit. It seemed to be a very nice one to me. The first day I wore it to the office, Hub Kelly, one of our senior salesmen, bellowed across the room, "My Gawd, look what Diehl's wearing!" All eyes turned toward me and there were a few chuckles. Hub laughed, "What time is the first race at Northville, Red?" I got the message: "We" wear more conservative colors. That suit was used for social events, but seldom again for business.

My Bethlehem Steel sales "uniform" simply was too conservative for social events, and so I have always had two wardrobes—one for business and one for after hours. I have always been annoyed by that fact, but for me it was an issue not worth fighting about.

The Bethlehem Steel uniform would not be acceptable for a college professor or a social worker. They have their own uniforms. But it has also been interesting to observe that the Bethlehem Steel sales uniform has always brought me better attention on airlines, in stores, banks, restaurants, and professional offices than does my sport coat. Having served on a number of boards of directors, it is clear to me that boards of conservative institutions and businesses expect conservative dress, while boards of social service agencies do not.

Mind you, there is no written code for all this. It is part of a process of identification, and the pressures are definitely there for people to conform to the agreed-upon style of dress.

As one moves up in many companies, there are pressures on where to live. Certain sections of town are the "right" areas, and certain schools are the "best." More than one Bethlehem Steel executive, following a promotion, has moved into the posh Saucon Valley area from a perfectly fine home just a few miles away simply because it was the area where many associates of his equivalent status lived.

There are subtle pressures to read the same magazines and newspapers. It was always safe for me to quote from the *Wall Street Journal*. The *New York Times* was sometimes suspect because of its liberal editorial stance. Philadelphia papers were for people with no taste; don't quote them. Most business, sports, and news magazines were in. Definitely out were literary magazines and those dealing with social issues.

Believe it or not, there is even such a thing as a drink code. Certain cocktails are okay at certain times. Bloody Marys and Screwdrivers are okay as "eye-openers," but never after dinner. Certain drinks are never in order. Any aspiring young executive who goes out with his boss and orders a "seven and seven" or a "rum and coke" is sealing his or her own doom. There are even "in" brands of scotch, bourbon, gin, and vodka. The "in" person *always* specifies his or her brand when ordering.

Pressures can be present for after-hours interests also. If the Chairman of the Board is an avid golfer, there will be many executives playing golf. If he likes the racquet sports, others will, too. It has been interesting to observe during my career at Bethlehem Steel how interest in sports tended to follow the tastes of the top management. If certain local charities are supported by members of top management, or if their wives are heads of fund-raising drives, it is as certain as the sun will rise that others in the company will have similar interests.

With so many subtle and not-so-subtle pressures existing within many organizations, it should surprise no one that there comes to be a sharing of values also. There tends to be a conformity as to what things in life are important, what ideologies are to be supported, what issues are of concern, and even what political parties or candidates are to be supported. The management of many corporations is not

averse to letting the workers know its position on certain pieces of
legislation and which political party most favors this self-interest.
With the legitimization of corporate political action committees, there
is considerable pressure exerted on employees to contribute (anony-
mously) to PAC funds.

The pressures to conform exist in varying forms and degrees in
every job. Taken by themselves, they may not present any problems
for most of us. They are usually too insignificant to fuss about. But
collectively, these pressures can be the means for the total surrender
of a human being to the principality of occupation.

Saying No

To do justice to any job, there must be a commitment of time,
energy, and loyalty. We owe such commitments to our work if we are
to be responsible. If one works within an organization, there will be
pressures to "fit in" with the practices, styles, and values of the
group. If we are to be responsible, we will have to accept and participate in a certain amount of such conformity. The key question at all
times is: Who is in control? Am I in control and making conscious
decisions about my involvement in my job, or is the job controlling me?

It seems to me that in order to keep from being victimized by our
jobs, we need to check ourselves at certain points and, when appropriate, say no. The "no" may be to a request to forego a planned
family event because of something unexpected on the job. It may be a
"no" to working overtime. It may be a refusal to conform to some
practice of the group.

There came a time in my career at Bethlehem Steel when I felt a
need to find out if the company owned me. I had been able to say no to
some minor issues, but I had a nagging feeling that I was kidding
myself about my freedom. In 1951, the company moved us, with two
small babies, to Detroit. In 1959, the company moved us, with four
small children, to Bethlehem. In 1961, the company moved us to
Philadelphia. In each case, it was a promotion, an advancement, and
meant more money. Each time we moved, Judy and the children had
to start their lives all over again. I had a built-in support system
awaiting me when I transferred in the form of a group of Bethlehem

Steel associates. But that was not so for Judy and the children. They always had to start from scratch.

I began to question myself as to whether I would go anywhere I was asked to go. Would I always say yes? Would the family always have to make the sacrifice in favor of the company?

And so it was in 1967 that I got the word that our senior vice-president wanted to see me. I pretty well knew what that meant, and my personal intelligence network confirmed that I was to be offered a sales manager's job. That would involve another move.

At that time, our two oldest children were in high school. The 1960s were tough years for young people. The Vietnam war was heating up, there was social protest all over the country, and the drug culture was thriving. Our children were handling those years remarkably well. I could only imagine what it would mean to them personally to have to start all over again in the middle of a high-school career and in a new town. I concluded that this was the time for me to say no.

Driving to our home office that morning, I wasn't sure if I had the courage to stick to my plan to turn the job down. There would be considerable pressure on me to take it, and there was a real likelihood that I would never again get an offer for advancement. Would I be content to stay in the job I had as an assistant manager for twenty more years?

My senior vice-president was a no-nonsense person. He got right to the point and told me I was going to be made sales manager of a division. He said that the general manager of that division had specifically requested me and that he agreed I was the best man for the job. He was all ready to call in the general manager who was waiting in an adjoining office when I told him that, for family reasons, I could not take the job.

He was dumbfounded. No one turns down such opportunities, he pointed out. He reminded me that I would be the youngest sales manager in the company and that my future with Bethlehem Steel was very bright. I stood my ground, but as a minor concession to him, I agreed to think it over for twenty-four hours. When I left that office, however, both of us knew what my ultimate answer would be.

I drove home that day with a kind of freedom that I have seldom experienced. I had said no! I had said it when the stakes were very high. I knew that day that the company did not own me, nor would it ever. I was free!

That single experience gave me a degree of confidence during my remaining years with the company that my actions and decisions were not being influenced by any personal ambitions to get ahead. When I later did get another offer to become a sales manager, I was able to take the job, knowing the company did not own me.

Indications are that more people are saying no on some major issues involving their jobs. For the past five years, it has become increasingly difficult for major corporations to get people to transfer to other cities. Part of the reason is financial. Considering the cost of buying and financing a new home and considering the higher income tax brackets that people are moving into, there is no longer much of a financial incentive. With an increasing number of both husbands and wives working, there is also the problem of resolving which of the partners must give up a job and start anew at the next location.

More than this, younger people are more individualistic. The bad side of this individualism is a tendency to be self-centered and anti-authoritarian. On the good side, it does mean they are less likely to sell their souls to the company.

Louis Banks, former managing editor of *Fortune* and currently an adjunct professor of management at MIT, in his article "Here Come the Individualists" in *Harvard Magazine* (September-October 1977), states:

> I would argue that the strongest trend at work today in American life is the rise of a kind of popular individualism and nowhere does it manifest itself more clearly than at the boundary line between the bright, youthful executive (male or female) and the traditional expectations of corporate bosses. Whereas in the long march of corporate growth following World War II we lived in a period of business dominance *in its own terms,* we are now entering a period of individualism in *its own terms.* In my view, this is not an anti-business or anti-organization trend per se. But it will demand accommodation between conventional business values and individual values of a scope and kind we have never quite seen before.

Such a trend may be all for the good, both for the individuals and the company. But before we celebrate this shift too much, we need to remind ourselves that what is really happening is that young people are moving away from the dominance of the principality of occupation toward a dominance of the power of individualism. Either can be demonic.

This chapter has had a heavy focus on occupation in the corporate structure. It is the area in which I have the greatest first-hand experience. I feel, however, that the forces I've identified are at work in all types of occupations.

We all know mothers and homemakers who are workaholics, who invest massive quantities of energy in their occupation, and who are so totally dedicated to their home and family that they have scarcely any outside interests. They, too, feel pressures to conform to the styles and values which their group tends to adopt. Their children should be neat, clean, and well-behaved. Homes should be orderly at all times, and spotless. They should be good cooks and, along with everything else, they should keep young, trim, and attractive. Like the corporate executives, these mothers can be so totally hooked by their occupation that they, too, suffer depression called the "empty nest syndrome" when their children leave home.

The principality we call our job is a powerful one. It has a voracious appetite. It will gladly consume all of us if we allow it. But if we keep in mind that as Christians we are in the world but not of it, and that we are a totally liberated people, we can carry out our priestly calling to serve responsibly through our occupation without becoming captives of it.

NOTES—CHAPTER 6

1. Earl Shorris, *The Oppressed Middle: Politics of Middle Management* (Garden City, N.Y.: Doubleday, 1981).

7

Institutions

Johnstown, Pennsylvania was hit by a devastating flood early in the morning, July 20, 1977. Since I missed the morning news on my way to work, the first reports I received of the flood came from people in the office. Information was sketchy. Later in the day, all of the managers in our central headquarters were called to attend a nation-wide conference call with all our district sales offices to get a briefing on the flood situation. The company has a major steel plant in Johnstown.

The vice-president who conducted the meeting began by describing the six-inch rainfall which deluged the area and the twelve-foot wall of water which cascaded through the valley, bringing heavy destruction to many areas. "Although there was little warning," he said, "it appears our people had enough time to bank the blast furnaces, tap the open hearths, and push all the coke out of the ovens." I heard a few whispers of relief in the room. Apparently the most expensive equipment was saved from more serious damage.

However, as the report continued, it was apparent that our rolling mills, our railroad car assembly shop, and almost every other facility was under water. That was bad news. The vice-president went on, "Two of our mines have been flooded, and two more are without power." That wasn't so good, either. "Fortunately," he continued, "it appears that there was no loss of life in the plant. Some workers are stranded, but no one has been killed." Good, I thought. Then continued a list of instructions about not trying to contact the plant and being patient to learn details of how individual customers' orders would be affected.

As the meeting closed and we walked toward the elevators, I recall that several of us lamented that the flood was one more of an unfortunate series of events that had plagued our company. "Isn't there ever going to be any good news?" groaned one of my associates.

It was not until I got home that evening, read the newspapers, and saw the evening news on television that I learned of the devastation in that little valley. Houses had been overturned, mobile homes swept away, bridges destroyed, and scores of people were dead with hundreds still missing. When the waters would recede, these people would return to their homes, stores, and offices to see most of their life's possessions ruined. It was tragic.

As I sat there watching the television, I was struck with the realization that in the conference call earlier in the day, there was nothing said about the destruction and death outside our plant. The entire meeting focused on how our plant and the employees within that plant had been affected. Not for one moment in that meeting had it occurred to me or to anyone else to ask how serious things were *outside* our plant. While I had felt relief that none of our people inside the plant had been killed, it never occurred to me that quite possibly there had been loss of life in the *families* of our employees. Nor had I thought far enough to realize that while these plant employees were struggling to save our equipment, at the same time they were experiencing severe loss as their homes were being destroyed.

There it was again—my institutional myopia. It was just another example of how easy it is for me and others to be so absorbed in our functions within an organization that we lose sight of what is going on outside.

My associates and I are generally compassionate people. We volunteer time and talents in community and church service. We contribute money to charitable causes. We hurt when we see others hurting. Why is it that the vision of basically good people can so easily be narrowed by the interests of the institution they serve?

It would be wrong to suggest that institutional myopia exists only in business and industry. Far from it. It can arise wherever people come together in an organizational enterprise.

Have you ever taken an injured person to the emergency floor of a hospital and found that there seemed to be more concern about getting admission forms filled out and insurance identification established than there was about the victim's pain? If there is blood spilling on the floor, admission is generally faster—not necessarily because of compassion, but quite often because it represents a clean-up job for someone.

I am on the board of directors of several community service agencies. Each agency has a special field of interest, and it is easy to ignore the whole person as we try to meet some particular need of a client. Our vision is narrowed.

Institutional myopia exists within the church. It was interesting to read a small article about the Johnstown flood in the August issue of our church magazine, *The Lutheran*. After relating how the Central Pennsylvania Synod of our church was helping with relief efforts, the article gave a short assessment of the destruction: "Early reports indicated that at least 40 people were killed and more than 400 were missing in the wake of the flood. At least one Lutheran Church in America congregation—First, in the community's downtown—sustained flood damage, but synod officials initially indicated the homes of Lutheran families were harder hit than the churches."

Well, I thought, the church's vision of the Johnstown flood isn't much broader than that of Bethlehem Steel. Perhaps a Presbyterian or Baptist or Roman Catholic building was completely destroyed, but we'll never know about it by reading that article. And was it *only* the homes of Lutheran families which were "harder hit than the churches," or could it be that a few Methodists and Jews and even some atheists lost everything? How much broader a view could have been given if the report stated, "but synod officials initially indicated that the homes of the people were harder hit than the public buildings."

A Multitude of Organizations

Human beings are social creatures. To get things done and to meet our need to belong, we have created an incredible number of organizations and institutions. So that there can be order in our society, we have structured a political system consisting of nations, states, counties, cities, towns, boroughs, villages, and so on. Within these political units there are departments, divisions, commissions, authorities, boards, offices, and auxiliaries. Each political unit and sub-unit has a life of its own which continues as members come and go.

There are a wide variety of organizations associated with our occupations: labor unions, chambers of commerce, trade associations, professional associations, and the like. Many of these organizations are national in scope and are subdivided into state and local chapters, each of which is an organization in itself.

There is a long list of service and character-building organizations that also have national, state, and local sub-units (Kiwanis, Rotary, Lions, the YMCA and YWCA, Boy Scouts, Girl Scouts, Indian Guides, Alcoholics Anonymous, Big Brothers), human service organizations (United Way, Red Cross, Cancer Society), and sports organizations (Little Leagues, N.C.A.A., National Bowling Congress, Professional Golf Association, National Football League, National Rifle Association). There are national, state, and sometimes local structures for some of the issue-oriented movements in our nation—The National Association for the Advancement of Colored People, The American Civil Liberties Union, Common Cause, the National Organization for Women, Planned Parenthood, Gray Panthers, and others. There are social and fraternal organizations such as the Elks, Eastern Star, Shriners, college sororities and fraternities, the Ku Klux Klan, and various ethnic associations. Our religious denominations—the Roman Catholics, Lutherans, Presbyterians, Baptists, Methodists, Episcopalians, Moravians, Mennonites, Quakers, and others—have national, regional, and local units. Our political parties have state and national divisions.

So far, we have only considered *national* organizations. In addition, there are tens of thousands of local clubs, associations, and institutions which are flourishing. Consider them—golf and country clubs, swim clubs, tennis clubs, flower and garden clubs, investment clubs, bridge clubs, dance clubs, singles clubs, sports leagues, stamp clubs, antique car clubs, hiking clubs, ski clubs, theater clubs, music groups—the list is mind-boggling.

Without belaboring the point, there are a fantastic number of organizations and institutions in our country. Each and every one of them have their own existence, personality, and mode of life. These organizations are not simply the sum total of their members, but live and grow and sometimes die totally apart from the living and growing and dying of their members. They are truly principalities.

Just as our occupations demand time, energy, and loyalty from us, so do all the other organizations and institutions with which we associate. They are voracious and care not about our individual welfare, for they will gladly accept *all* of our time, *all* of our energy, and our *total* loyalty if we care to commit ourselves to that degree. We do know people, do we not, whose lives revolve around a club or association or movement to the virtual exclusion of everything else, including family?

Because all organizations want our total commitment, they compete among themselves for our attention. William Stringfellow explains:

> Men are veritably besieged, on all sides, at every moment simultaneously by these claims and strivings of the various powers, each seeking to dominate, usurp or take a person's time, attention, abilities, effort; each grasping at life itself, each demanding idolatrous service and loyalty. In such tumult, it becomes very difficult for a human being even to identify the idols which would possess him.[1]

Can we identify the idols which would possess us? Are we aware of their sales pitch?

Some of the organizations which invite our commitment are pretty much up front in their sales pitch. If one decides to join the local tennis club, it is largely in one's own self-interest. In return for the investment of time and energy, one will learn to play tennis, get some exercise, and perhaps enlarge one's social circle. Yes, it is possible to "get hooked" on tennis, but the decision to increase or decrease commitment is still essentially one of self-interest.

But there are organizations which lay claim to higher purposes—which exist to advance an ideology, promote the welfare of society, bring "truth" to humankind, or serve the cause of righteousness. These organizations can have a more diabolical approach. Instead of appealing to self-interest, they speak of self-sacrifice. Instead of being for one's own good, they claim to be for the good of all. Disengagement from such organizations is more difficult because they can so easily make us feel guilty. It is much easier to reduce a commitment to the tennis club than to Meals on Wheels—simply because the latter so badly "needs" us.

It is paradoxical that those organizations in our society which lay claim to noble objectives also have a high potential for being destructive. When one is totally possessed by a cause, an ideology, a religion, or a worthy movement, one becomes so zealous that fanaticism can easily develop. The possessed one becomes convinced that there can be only one cause, one ideology, one revealed truth.

On the other hand, it is also a paradox that real social change seldom comes about without the efforts or leadership of a fanatic. The abolition of slavery in the United States in the 1860s owes much to the fanaticism of William Lloyd Garrison. The German National Social movement of the 1940s, which ultimately resulted in the genocide of six million Jews, was due to the fanaticism of Adolf Hitler.

The fanatic can be a dangerous person because he or she is a person with deep psychological needs. Eric Hoffer, in *The True Believer,* describes the fanatic:

> The fanatic is perpetually incomplete and insecure. He cannot generate self-assurance out of his own resources—out of his rejected self—but finds it only in clinging passionately to whatever support he happens to embrace. This passionate attachment is the essence of his blind devotion and religiosity, and he sees in it the source of all virtue and strength. Though his single-minded dedication is a holding on for dear life, he easily sees himself as the supporter and defender of the holy cause to which he clings. And he is ready to sacrifice his life to demonstrate to himself and others that such, indeed, is his role. He sacrifices his life to prove his worth.[2]

As Christians, we witness to a belief that none of us can prove our worth before God. It is only through God's gracious gift of love and acceptance that we have an assurance that we are worthy. The person who believes that self-worth is proved through commitment to a cause is a person who has been possessed by a demonic power.

Since organizations which exist for the primary cause of serving others can be treacherous, it would be well to think about three of them.

Political Organizations

Perhaps no constellation of organizations is as wild and woolly as those connected with the political structures of our country—our legislatures, commissions, political parties. The underlying purpose of our political organizations is to provide for the general welfare of society. This is the banner under which all of the individuals and groups which operate within our political structure can claim legitimacy.

Having such a noble purpose, it is strange that no other institution of American society consistently ranks at the bottom of public esteem as does "politics." Politics has become a dirty word, a word to describe human interaction of the most self-serving nature.

That general disdain for politics and politicians has persisted in our nation is indeed unfortunate. Undoubtedly, it has caused some "men who have greatness within them," to borrow a phrase from Albert Camus, to decide not to go into public life. However, since political structures have such a strong influence in our society, it is important that Christians respond to the need for intelligent and responsible participation in the political process.

Writing in *Christians with Secular Power,* Mark Gibbs quotes David Owen, the former British Foreign Secretary, as saying that it is the calling, the burden of politicians, to "muddy their hands" on behalf of the rest of the country—to which Gibbs adds, "It is precisely for this that we must honor and support our fellow Christians who are involved in politics."[3]

In my opinion, politics is muddy because it is the battleground on which so many principalities and powers contest for domination. Our political parties compete for domination of our governmental structures. The institutions of government assert this domination by passing laws, enforcing laws, and punishing law breakers. Our judicial institutions assert their domination by judging people, judging disputes, and judging laws. The political arena also is the place where many of our ideologies compete for support—federalism, states' rights, capitalism, socialism, civil liberties, environmentalism, and countless others.

While it is important that Christians not avoid participating in political organizations, it is essential that they recognize and understand the treacherous forces which seek to dominate them in the process.

It has been interesting to observe the kinds of principalities which have moved in on my wife, Judy, since she began her career in public office some six years ago. First, there is the political party. Even though the influence of political parties has waned in recent years, it is still important to have your party organization supporting you. You get that support either by (1) being a loyal worker for the party and having it support you in a primary election or (2) defeating the party's candidate in a primary election. Since Judy was a newcomer and a woman, there was no chance she would get the party's endorsement for a primary election. So she had to run all alone and in opposition to the favored party candidate. This is difficult, since primary elections do not draw high voter turnout, and those who do vote are the party loyalists who will follow party suggestions.

By hard work and with good credentials, Judy beat the party nominee in the primary runoff. Immediately, the party chairman got in touch with her and discussions began concerning the campaign for the fall election. The principality of the party which had been foe a few days before had suddenly become friend.

Judy instantly had to make choices as to how much the party should dictate her campaign and how much she should control. Who would decide where she would appear? Who would represent her position on issues? What would be her position on party issues? Who would represent her to the newspapers? While the party chairman was careful not to overwhelm her, it was obvious to us that, given free rein, the party organization would gladly have dominated Judy and her campaign.

In her first year as a county commissioner, she came face to face with the games that are played. On some issues, other commissioners would play to the galleries for future votes. Some would pose as "noncompromisers" on certain issues to gain the mantle of purity. Some would offer to trade votes between certain bills. Some would not do their homework and would speak and vote out of sheer ignorance. In all of these circumstances, Judy had to decide what was important and what was not; when to speak up and when to let things pass. She could afford to let the unimportant "game playing" pass, but there were times when she felt she had to say no to the pressures to play along.

To have witnessed this process firsthand at a local level has given me a great deal more sympathy and understanding for our state and national political leaders who are subject to much stronger pressures and have many more issues to face.

A recent development within our American political system has made things even more difficult for those who would try to walk a responsible path through a maze of competing pressures. It is the rise of single-issue politics. This kind of politics has been steadily growing to the point where in 1976, a presidential election year, more people contributed money to special interest groups than to the Democratic and Republican parties combined.

Single-issue political movements such as "No Nukes," "Save the Dolphins," "Right to Life," "Right to Choice," "Gun Control," and many, many others certainly have their place in American society. But they must be recognized for what they are—movements, organizations, powers, if you will, which take on a life of their own, which grow and seek greater dominion over people and which, ultimately, can be demonic.

The demonic nature of special-interest groups and single-issue politics can be clearly seen when the supporters of these movements judge their political leaders *solely* on their position regarding their pet issue. It is incredible to see groups, especially those who claim to be Christian, seeking to destroy capable, hardworking, dedicated legislators simply because they voted the "wrong way" on their special issue. Writing in the October 8, 1980 issue of *The Christian Century* prior to the election of Ronald Reagan, Robert Zwier and Richard Smith pointed out the narrow-mindedness of mind of the conservative Christian political organizations:

> The legislative ratings presented by these groups are flawed. They presume, on the basis of from ten to fifteen votes, to issue final judgments about the morality of individual legislators. In so doing, they again claim that the will of God is bound up with one particular position on very complex issues of national policy. Something is clearly amiss when *Christian Voice* gives the lowest possible rating to a Baptist minister (William Gray) and to a Catholic priest (Robert Drinan) while giving the highest score to a congressman who has been indicted in the Abscam scandal (Richard Kelly).

We have experienced the situation in our country where good people have been defeated because of their position on one issue. The purveyors of single-issue politics have tasted that blood, and they openly declare they are out for more. They would claim that they are driven by the Word of God or the cause of humanity. In truth, they have become possessed by a demon organization.

Social Service Organizations

For a number of years, I have been on the board of the Lehigh Valley Community Council, and in the past year, I was its president. The mission of the Community Council is to be the catalyst for the planning and coordination of all human services in a tri-county area. There are about two hundred agencies and organizations which are members of the Community Council; some are direct providers of human services and some are organizations with an overall concern for the welfare of our tri-county area.

While all our member agencies and organizations agree that there should be comprehensive planning and coordination of human services, in actual fact each member organization is primarily interested in its own mission. For example, the staff and board of an agency dealing with, let us say, the teenage drug problem, sees its work as highly critical. When they go before the allocations committee of the United Way, they are absolutely convinced that they are more worthy of funds than any other agency. Every staff person and every board member of every agency feels just as strongly about the worthiness of his or her organization. It is not that people are narrow-minded or ignorant or prejudiced; they are broad-minded, intelligent, open people. But the nature of the organization is that when one commits time, energy, and loyalty to it, one buys into its purpose. It has been my observation that when the purpose is a worthy one, as in caring about drugs among our youth, the level of commitment can readily be raised. So with each human service agency having a very high commitment to its own mission, it is almost impossible to plan and coordinate a comprehensive human service system. In a sense, the overall welfare of the community suffers because of the passion of each organization committed to serving the community. I have even seen decent, honorable people cheat on behalf of their institutions—in social services as well as business.

A few years ago, as a board member of a social service agency, I sat through a budget-setting meeting. This particular agency received a large share of its funds from the federal government channeled through one of our state's departments of human welfare. We had drawn up a budget which called for a slight increase of federal funds, mostly as the result of creeping inflation. But the agency's staff director was concerned about the fact that because of some delays in the implementation of a current program, we had not spent our full allocation for the current year. He quite properly pointed out that it would be difficult to secure even a modest increase in our budget for next year when we had not even used up our current allocation of funds. Moreover, the regulations provided that there could be no carry-over of unspent funds from one year to the next. Money not spent would have to be returned to Harrisburg. So the suggestion was made that by juggling our accounting, that is, by transferring unused funds from one program into another which lent itself to some pre-spending, and by prepurchasing equipment and supplies for the next year, we could spend all our current year funds. This would, it was pointed out, give us a better chance at securing an increased alloca-tion for next year; it would give us a jump on expenditures for next year; and it would mean we wouldn't have to return any money to Harrisburg.

The suggestion sounded very good to most of the people. The issue of responsibility bothered me. I asked if they didn't feel we had a responsibility to our federal government to send the money back if we didn't use it. Staff members quickly pointed out that what we were doing was really just a part of the game that is played with all funding proposals—even in business, they added. While the board members did acknowledge a degree of responsibility towards the source of our funds, their commitment to the agency itself was higher. I do not think any of these people would have considered a similar tactic of shifting their personal funds to get around the federal government. But the commitment to the institution was so great that they were will-ing to bend a personal ethic for the sake of the well-being of their organization.

Religious Organizations

Religious organizations are by no means exempt from the list of principalities which seek to dominate us. They do seem to enjoy a special status, however. Except for some of the extreme off-beat religious sects, most Christians grant our religious organizations a degree of respect and deference of which, perhaps, they are un-worthy.

First, we need to define the terms. It is said that the Christian church is the living body of Christ. That definition does not have in mind the various denominations of churches or the divisions and congregations within them. No, the Christian church is that mystical body of believers which has existed in various forms and places ever since that first Easter morning. The Christian church is even more than the sum total of all the members of all the religious organizations which claim allegiance to Jesus Christ.

The religious organizations being dealt with here are the various institutional groupings which have developed as the Christian faith grew and spread. It is amazing how religious organizations have proliferated over the centuries.

I am a member of a congregation—a religious organization. Our congregation is a member of a national denomination—a religious organization. Our congregation is also a member of a cluster of local congregations and a member of a district subgroup of our national church body. In addition to our national organization, there are several other national Lutheran denominations in the United States, and they work together through the Lutheran Council in the USA. Furthermore, Lutherans around the world come together in an organization known as the Lutheran World Federation.

Other denominations have their own local, regional, national, and international organizations. Moreover, there are large numbers of ecumenical religious organizations—councils of churches at local, state, and national levels. In these religious organizations, the powers and principalities are alive and well today.

The local congregation is not supposed to be terminal in God's purpose; it is supposed to be instrumental. It is not supposed to exist as an end in itself, but as a means to an end. The local congregation is the place where the people of God gather around Word and Sacrament, for praise and prayer, for education and fellowship, and for stimulation and support *so that* they can scatter into the world on Monday as priests, being the channel for God's interaction with the world.

Unfortunately and almost without exception, local congregations are so concerned with the busywork of the organization, with preparing for the gathering of the faithful on Sunday morning, with the raising of funds, with the enlisting of volunteers, with choir practice, with committee meetings and clean-up, fix-up, paint-up projects,

that there is scarcely any time, energy, or concern left for the equipping of the members for their priestly roles in the world. There is an
assumption that if eveything goes well on a Sunday morning, the
people of God will automatically carry out their ministries in the
world during the rest of the week. How can an organization which
spends ninety-nine percent of its time and energy on maintaining the
institution possibly expect that, during a one-hour worship service,
its people will come to know that *their* real purpose is to be spending
ninety-nine percent of their time being God's agents of love and
reconciliation in the world? It should be obvious to all of us that our
assumption is false.

Like the principalities of occupation, the principality of the religious organization demands time, energy, and loyalty. Moveover,
like other principalities, it will gladly and greedily accept our total
commitment of time, energy, and loyalty. How many of us know
people who have left their church because of being burned out? They
were so willing to help that endless tasks and responsibilities were
loaded on them until they could take no more. The scandal is that
these believers came with the expectation of serving God and walking
with him, yet they really ended up serving another organization.

A number of years ago while I was serving on the national Executive Council of our denomination, an incident occurred which clearly
illustrates how the needs of the institution can frustrate the mission of
the church. Part of our three-day agenda called for us to approve some
changes in the approved constitution for congregations. This is a
defined responsibility of the Executive Council. In leading us through
these changes, the secretary of the church pointed out that certain
sections pertaining to congregational structure had optional provisions. These optional provisions were noted in brackets. The text of
the constitution, however, also had clarifying phrases, but these were
noted in parentheses. It was important, the secretary said, that the
revised constitution not use parentheses where brackets were intended because the brackets referred to optional provisions, not to
clarification. As we worked our way through the revisions, there were
several points at which there was a debate as to whether brackets or
parentheses should be used.

Frankly, all of this bored me. My eyes started wandering and soon fell upon the copy of the *New York Times* which I had thrown on the floor next to my chair. There in bold headlines were the words, "Nixon Resumes Bombing of Hanoi." It was that period in our Vietnam peace efforts in which President Nixon, unable to persuade the North Vietnamese to resume peace talks with us, had decided to try to "bomb them back to the peace table." I looked at those headlines and felt sick. Here in this room were thirty-three members of the national Executive Council of one of the nation's largest Christian denominations, debating whether certain words in a document should be in brackets or parentheses—while outside in the world our nation was bombing the hell out of Hanoi as a means of resuming peace talks.

It was more than I could bear. I raised my hand. The secretary recognized me. I said something to the effect that it was upsetting to me that we, the leadership of our church, should be debating punctuation in a constitution while at that very moment our airplanes were blasting civilians in Hanoi on behalf of peace. I reminded my associates how divided our people were on the issue of this war.

"Isn't there any connection between what we do in this room and what goes on in the outside world?" I asked.

There was silence, embarrassed silence. No one said a word for about twenty seconds. No one knew what to say. I had thrown a nasty question into our institutional agenda.

The poor secretary was on the spot. After it appeared that no one wanted to respond to my question, he cleared his throat and said, "Do I take it from the silence that we want to continue with the constitution?"

One hand went up. It was that of one of our most distinguished theologians.

"Dr. Stendahl?" said the secretary.

"No, I think not," he said. "I think we need to talk about how this body does relate to what is happening in Southeast Asia at this moment. I move we put brackets and parentheses aside for the time being and talk about Mr. Diehl's question."

So began a spirited discussion of how the Lutheran Church in America should be responding to and supporting peace efforts. Out of that discussion came a pastoral letter from the president of the church

to all of our clergy, presenting various sides of the national dilemma
but encouraging them to engage their members in conversation about
the situation and in prayer for an end to the war.

The principality of church organization was thus temporarily frus-
trated. But not for too long. We eventually took care of the brackets
and parentheses. Principalities don't give up that easily.

In *The Screwtape Letters,* C. S. Lewis has Screwtape, the senior
devil, advising Wormwood, his agent on earth, on the ways to possess
the Christian. In one of the letters, Screwtape tells Wormwood:

> One of our greatest allies at present is the church itself. Do not misunder-
> stand me. I do not mean the church as we see her spread out through all
> time and space and rooted in eternity, terrible as an army with banners.
> That, I confess, is a spectacle which makes our boldest tempters uneasy.
> But fortunately it is quite invisible to these humans.[4]

Perhaps Screwtape overstates the case when he says that the
church, the body of Christ, is "quite invisible to these humans." For
me, it is proof of the power of the Holy Spirit that somehow through
all of the busy work of serving the institution, the liberating power of
the gospel does break through and change the lives of people. But
Screwtape is right in suggesting that religious organizations constitute
one of the most fertile hunting grounds for the demonic principalities
and powers of our culture.

Whether it be political, social service, or religious organizations,
the spirit of a demonic principality is ever present. We need to
recognize the powers of our organizations for what they are. They all
can be dangerous, but perhaps the most treacherous ones are those
which beguile and charm us with their lofty purposes.

NOTES—CHAPTER 7

1. William Stringfellow, *An Ethic for Christians and Other Aliens in a
Strange Land* (Waco: Word Books, 1973), p. 94.

2. Eric Hoffer, *The True Believer* (New York: Harper and Row, 1951),
p. 83.

3. Mark Gibbs, *Christians with Secular Power* (Philadelphia: Fortress
Press, 1981), pp. 64–65.

4. C. S. Lewis, *The Screwtape Letters* (Philadelphia: Fortress Press,
1980), pp. 14–15.

8

Security

"I sure admire what you are doing," he said. "It takes a helluva lot of courage." We were talking about my decision to leave Bethlehem Steel for a new career in my own company.

"Oh, I don't know," I said modestly. "After all, Jennifer is in her last year of college, so our financial responsibilities to our children have been fulfilled. We have virtually paid off the mortgage on our home. It's much larger than we need, so we're thinking of selling it and moving into a smaller house in town. We can get by with a much lower standard of living."

"Well," he said, "the idea of starting a new career has a lot of appeal to me, too. I know exactly what I'd do."

"What's that?" I asked.

"I'd get into the house restoration business. I like to restore old things, especially homes. You know, we've done it with our present home."

"Hey, you'd be good at that! Your home is just a jewel of a place. Why don't you take early retirement, too?"

"I think it's too risky. The way inflation is running wild, who knows what a dollar will be worth ten years from now? At least here I'll get raises to keep me even with inflation."

"Yes," I said, "but you could make good money with your home restoration business. You probably would make out even better financially than you're doing now."

"Unless a depression came along," he added. "I'm afraid that in trying to control inflation, we're going to end up with a major depression. In that case, no one will be in the market for a restored home." He shook his head. "It's just too risky a time."

Here was a man slightly over sixty who had a dream of doing something different in his life, but who was afraid to leave his present security. His home was paid off, his children were married and on their own, he owned other real estate, had two expensive cars and a boat, regularly vacationed in the Caribbean, was a member of the country club, and was earning a six-figure salary. Yet he felt it was "too risky" to do something he had long wished to do.

How much security does a person need?

Abraham Maslow, one of the most quoted psychologists in the field of human motivation, many years ago presented us with his "hierarchy of needs." This classic concept is based on Maslow's conviction that all humans have the same kinds of needs and, as the primary needs are satisfied, higher ones emerge. At the bottom of his hierarchy are the physiological needs—food, water, clothing, and shelter. When these basic requirements are met, the human then must satisfy "safety needs." These include such things as security, stability, protection, law and order, freedom from fear, freedom from anxiety, and so on. In short, the human wants to make certain that the basic physiological needs will continue to be met.

Maslow lists love and belonging as a third level of needs. The human will seek relationships of affection and identification with others, such as family, neighborhood, or community. At the fourth level, humans want esteem, that is, to have self-respect and the admiration of others. The highest human need is for self-actualization, that is, the person must be doing what he or she individually is best suited for.

Most psychologists would agree that security is a rather basic need for all of us. Because it is an important need, it has power over our lives. It controls what we do. As with my friend, security can be so powerful that it can keep us from doing what we would very much like to do. In fact, Maslow points out, an extreme obsession with security is really a neurosis.

Are we fully aware of the way the need for security can dominate our lives and keep us from being whole people? Many of us are not.

After I announced to management that I had decided to take early retirement and start a new career, I began to realize how much the need for security had taken over my life. Although I was able to convince myself intellectually that a change in careers would bring some stimulating new chapters into my life, and that I could swing it financially, my emotions said other things. For weeks, I would awaken in the morning with the same initial thought flashing through my mind: "Look, you enjoy your present work. You're near the peak of your earning capacity. You're well-respected in your field. And yet, you are leaving for something quite unknown. You must be crazy!" During the day, I would think through the decision to leave, reminding myself of all the new possibilities and convincing myself that the finances would work out. By evening, I was again feeling comfortable with the decision, that is, until the next morning.

The security fears began to subside until, from a financial analysis, it became apparent that I should defer any pension benefits for at least three years after retirement. Suddenly, I was looking at a total loss of income. How much could I earn in the new business I was about to start? I had no idea. Did we have enough in savings to carry us through those three years? Definitely not. How much income did we really need? What if one of our children had a financial emergency? What if my elderly mother needed expensive medical attention? The questions and fears swirled around me.

The power of security challenged me on the basis of responsibility. Was I really being a responsible person? Would it not be more responsible to hang in with that well-paying, high-esteem, secure job—at least for three more years? After all, my vice-president had indicated he would be happy to have me change my mind and stay on. The way was open. Wouldn't it be more responsible to my family if I stayed?

Precisely because I had been giving much thought to the power of security, I determined that I had to make the change. The need for security was dominating my life, and I suspected that if I gave into it now, in three years there would be other valid reasons not to make a change. I would be forever a captive.

I did not deny my need for security. I understand and agree that it is a basic need. At issue was the *source* of my security. Was there no other security for me apart from my job at Bethlehem Steel? Could I find no security in my years of experience in management, in the talents I had developed in my life, in the awareness that we could live a much simpler life style, or in my conviction that somehow God does clothe the lilies of the field? It was apparent that my security was bound up in a specific job to a degree I had never realized. I was a captive of that power of security. I had to let go.

A growing concern for security has been noted in recent years among high school and college students. The *Wall Street Journal* (June 3, 1981) carried a front-page article on the values and attitudes of today's students. "Less inspired by social issues than students of the recent past," the *Journal* said, "most of today's high school teenagers appear more preoccupied with personal concerns. Their big worry has become how they will fare in 'real life'—the student catch phrase connoting the grown-up scramble for money, jobs, and security."

The concern for economic security and safety from bodily harm has driven many people into a "bunker" style of living. The increase in crime, particularly among those who must steal in order to feed a drug habit, has caused many of our citizens to fortify their homes with double locks and chains, burglar alarms, and guns. Sadly, many elderly people in our major cities are not able to walk through their neighborhoods in safety anymore. In any group of people today, there will be some who have been victims of burglaries or muggings or vandalism. It is much too common for us to dismiss. The reality is there.

Yet one has to ask if perhaps the fear is commensurate with the reality. We have friends who absolutely refuse to go to New York for fear of being mugged. But the odds weigh heavily against that ever happening to them. We have friends who have spent thousands of dollars on elaborate devices to discourage break-ins. Yet if they are asked what treasures they would first try to save should there be a fire, they will more frequently point to sentimental treasures such as family scrapbooks than to television sets, cameras, or even silverware.

Too often people are afraid to speak up when they see an injustice or even an illegal act committed on their jobs. They will rationalize that they fear loss of their job. One has to ask if their jobs are really that insecure. The expression "don't rock the boat" represents a wisdom which even deters people from making constructive suggestions to their supervisors. This fear has kept many a good idea from ever seeing the light of day.

The concern for security, however, is not confined to jobs or material possessions. Many of us want the security of order and predictability so badly that we oppose almost all forms of change. Since change frequently involves the unknown, we'd rather not risk what it might bring or take away. As a result, many of us resist new ideas, friends, foods, travels, and social patterns. If one listens carefully to the reasons why some people oppose the Equal Rights Amendment, the concerns are all related to fear—fear of drastic social change, fear of collapse of the family, fear of loss of power (for men), fear of independence (for some women), fear of the unknown.

On a national level, we have been trying to insure our security by means of newer and more devastating military hardware. Ever since the end of World War II, we and the Russians have been escalating our nuclear capability until, at this point, both sides possess the equivalent of fourteen and one-half tons of TNT for every man, woman, and child on the earth. Whatever one side does to improve its security is quickly matched by the other. Are we any more secure today from nuclear warfare than we were five years ago? Ten years ago? Yet we are committing vast amounts of our resources to continued rounds of armament escalation. Is there the slightest bit of evidence to suggest that we will be any more secure five years from now than we are today?

The words *safety* and *security* are seldom used in the Bible. When they are, it is frequently in the sense that security can be found only in God, not in earthly things. The wisdom of the Book of Proverbs serves as an example: "The fear of man lays a snare, but he who trusts in the Lord is safe" (Prov. 29:25). The Psalms have a constant theme, that "strength comes from the Lord," not from men.

Jesus frequently appealed to his flock not to be overly concerned about security. In Matthew 6, we hear him saying, "Do not lay up for yourselves treasures on earth," "do not be anxious about . . . what you shall eat or what you shall drink," and "Is not . . . the body more than clothing?" and "do not be anxious about tomorrow." Older versions of the Bible used to translate the words "anxious" as "give thought to." The newer translations are more to the point. We are not to ignore the bodily needs for food, water, clothing, and shelter while awaiting a heavenly Santa Claus who will provide these things for us.

We are to deal responsibly in this world with what we have, but we are not to be "anxious," that is, full of anxiety, about it all. We need to trust in the Lord who works through the creative orders which he has established. In the parable of the rich man who tore down his store houses to make room for larger ones, and then was called by God to surrender his life, Jesus concludes: "So is he who lays up treasure for himself, and is not rich toward God" (Luke 12:21). Finally, Jesus says: "For where your treasure is, there will your heart be also" (Luke 12:34).

This, of course, is the point. If our security needs are so strong that we cannot let go of a job or of material possessions, then that is where our heart resides. Then we are the victims of the power of security. If we are so insecure that we cannot bear change of any type, we are forever captives of that demonic power—security.

9

Power and Status

It is 7:15 A.M. A long black limousine makes its way down the street and turns into your driveway. You grab your briefcase and go to meet it.

"Good morning, Mr. Diehl!"

"Good morning, Nick. Looks like another nice day."

"Sure does!"

You climb in the back seat of the company limousine. On the seat next to you is the morning copy of the *Wall Street Journal*. You begin reading it as Nick points the car toward the airport.

Your car glides past the guardhouse at the gate, and friendly waves are exchanged between the security officer and your driver. The limousine flashes by the corporate hanger and makes its way onto the concrete apron where a company jet is waiting. The steward has noted the approach of the car and is ready to open the door for you.

"Good morning, Mr. Diehl. Can I take your briefcase?"

"Good morning, Paul. No, thanks, I can manage it. Am I the first one here?"

"Yes, you are, but I expect the others along any moment now. Grab yourself a seat. I've got your coffee waiting for you."

You climb the stairway to the cabin and step inside. A head pops out of the cockpit.

"Good morning, Mr. Diehl! It's a great day for flying!"

"Good morning, Ike. Glad to see you're our pilot today."

You pick one of the large upholstered swivel chairs and hand your jacket to the steward who is standing there with your coffee—made just the way you like it. You sit down and start reading the morning issue of the *New York Times* while awaiting the arrival of your business associates for the trip.

Such are the trappings of status. The scene just described happens every day to thousands of business and industry executives who "have arrived."

This chapter is being written in the library at Lehigh University at the same table where, as a student thirty-five years ago, I studied engineering. At that time, I would have been totally awed by the kinds of status given to me as I advanced through my career at Bethlehem Steel. Yet the status symbols accumulate so gradually and over a long enough period of time that one is not aware of the importance they assume in one's life. Status is one of those powers which can be demonic and possess us.

It feels good to be assigned your own private secretary, to have your office decorated in accordance with your wishes, to have your nameplate on the door, to have your own parking stall in the company garage, and to have the doorman greet you by name each morning and evening. It is impressive to have the locker room attendant at your own country club remember your children's names and ask about them. But it is even more impressive when the locker room attendant at a golf club where you have never played before greets you by name and takes you to a guest locker with your name on it. That's status.

You feel important repeatedly having lunch at the major businessmen's clubs all across the country—the Sky Club in New York, the Petroleum Club in Houston, or the Rainier Club in Seattle.

I recall the day that our New York sales manager and I had lunch with one of our customers at "21." As we were ushered to our table, our guest said, "Howdy, I'm very impressed." To which our manager modestly said, "Thank you." What I didn't realize then was that "21" and many other public and private restaurants have high-status tables which are held for very important people. The "in" people know which tables are which and respect the status they convey.

Status is next to the top in Abraham Maslow's hierarchy of needs. Once the basic physical needs have been met, once safety and security have been assured, and once one experiences affection and belonging, then the human being wants status. The powerful people have status. The elite have status.

The kind of power and status which I have experienced is that of the business world. But it exists in different forms in all areas of life. The academic community has its degrees, honors, titles, prestige positions, faculty dining rooms, reserved parking, and so on. The medical profession has labored long to achieve status in the community; ask any nurse how that status plays out in a hospital. Labor leaders have the problem of balancing enough status and power to impress management against the need to appear modest in the eyes of union membership. Certainly performing artists and sports heroes are awash with status symbols.

In business, the amount of status is usually in direct proportion to the power of the individual. Does the chairman of the board expend more calories per day than the shipping clerk or concentrate more than the accountant or make more decisions than the shop inspector? No. So why does he get more pay and have higher status? The answer: He wields greater power.

Of course, every now and then the little people will rise up to demonstrate their power. About a year ago, a major corporation announced it would be moving its corporate offices across the country. During an interview with the press, the board's chairman was asked if he expected that most of the employees would make the move. He said that he felt that most of the *important* employees would transfer, but secretaries and others would not. When the secretaries read in the paper the next day that they were not among the "important" employees, they decided to call attention to their importance by not answering any phones for one day. They did all of their other duties, but answered no phones. The turmoil which resulted from this demonstration of importance caused the board chairman to make a public apology.

Women in the business world can tap into the same power and status game as the men. The same rewards of money and perquisites are there, although not yet in equal degree. Some companies are so aggressively seeking women for management positions and helping them along that there is a degree of power for certain women today which comes just from being female.

Women in the home derive power and status from several directions. Being a homemaker and particularly a mother carries with it power and status in the eyes of the family. Unfortunately, in our materialistic society, the status of a mother is not held in as high esteem by many people as it should be. To be shaping the lives of children in the formative years means one has real power. This power and status is challenged by teenagers as they seek to establish their own freedom from the family. Sometimes it isn't until mothers are faced with the "empty nest" that they realize the power and status they have had.

Women also derive power and status from their husbands. If one is married to a man of power, the symbols are usually available to the wife as well. Country club memberships, large homes, flashy cars, expensive clothes, extended vacations, and the acquaintance of powerful people are status symbols for both husband and wife. In fact, many men of power find that their symbols can often be displayed better through their wives than by themselves. Most men of means cannot work *and* spend their time at the country club. Their status can be revealed, however, if their wives spend all their days at the club. Furthermore, women sometimes have greater opportunity to flaunt wealth through their manner of dress than men do.

The volunteer work of women in community service activities is another source of status. Every community has its hierarchy of causes and volunteer workers. Any woman who offers to drive for Meals on Wheels in our community will immediately be accepted as a volunteer. But not any woman will be accepted who offers to serve on one of the many committees for the annual Symphony Ball. Such work is usually undertaken by the elite. It is interesting to observe that if a woman of high status in the community decides to throw her energies behind a cause that has not had high visibility she alone can be responsible for increased community support. The boards of many community service agencies compete with each other to attract women of high status to their boards. And as so often happens, "them as has, gits."

One of the unfortunate results of this social pecking order in community service work is that women of high commitment and great ability frequently never get a chance to move into leadership positions. I have seen many instances in which women who have worked very hard and very effectively for a social service agency are passed over in favor of women with high social profiles when it comes time to elect board members or officers. And too often that social status is determined by the husband's position in the community. That's the way power works.

Status can be passed down through generations without the demonstration of power, provided there is wealth. When we lived on the Main Line of Philadelphia, there were a number of descendants of "old Philadelphia families" who were afforded status. They were not particularly active in business or community affairs. Their inherited wealth gave them status. However, if any such descendants were obviously without wealth, they were automatically also without status. Conversely, while newly acquired wealth may give the possessors some power, it does not immediately provide all the forms of status. Old wealth has more status than new wealth.

Some cultures bestow status upon age. Wisdom comes with age, and wisdom is power. But in America, age per se offers little status.

The ability of the musician, the artist, the writer, and the craftsperson provides status in many countries. But America tends to withhold such status until the talent has been demonstrated to have commercial appeal. An artist living off the benevolence of a patron does not have the status of an artist whose work is selling very well.

The propensity of America to relate status to wealth and economic success has been a constant source of irritation to the intellectual elite. Our intellectuals have raged and fumed over this for generations—at least those who have not won wealth in their own right. It has only been in recent years, however, that the scales of power have begun to tip more favorably towards the intellectuals. The post-World War II years saw an outpouring of college-educated people who were bored with the affluence of society. Their increased disenchantment with the elitism of money provided the intellectual community with its needed foot soldiers in its struggle for power.

Peter Berger describes the struggle between the two elitist groups this way:

> On the one side is the old elite of business enterprise, on the other side a new elite whose livelihood derives from the manipulation of symbols— intellectuals, educators, media people, members of the "helping professions" and a miscellany of planners and bureaucrats. This latter grouping has of late been called the "new class" in America—a not wholly felicitous term that is likely to stick for a while.[1]

In describing this "new class," Irving Kristol writes:

> They are not much interested in money, but heavily interested in power. Power for what? Well, the power to shape our civilization, a power which, in a capitalistic system, is supposed to reside in the free market. The "new class" wants to see much of this power redistributed to government, where *they* will then have a major say in how it is exercised.[2]

The power struggle between those who would wield power through our capitalistic system and those who would wield power through government was certainly evident in the election of Ronald Reagan. Candidate Reagan campaigned on a promise to "get big government off our backs." His first year in office has been marked by a significant shift in what has been the philosophy of government in the United States in recent decades. The relaxation of federal regulations in the areas of environmental concerns, consumer protection, occupational safety, health, and affirmative action are but a few examples. A reduction in funds for welfare programs and the shift from categorical grants administered by Washington to block grants administered by the states is a major change in philosophy.

Supporting candidate Reagan was a coalition of religious groups, commonly known as the Moral Majority. Led by a handful of television evangelists, these people called for a moral rebirth in America. Specifically, that meant being against abortion, against homosexuals, against equal rights for women, against gun control, against most welfare programs—and for prayer in the public schools, for increased armaments, for censorship of movies, books, and magazines, and for states' rights. It is more than coincidence that the position of the Moral Majority on each of these issues was directly opposite to that of the so-called "new class."

Peter Berger feels that much of the right-leaning evangelicalism "can in all likelihood be explained as a reaction against the power grab of the New Class."[3] If he is correct, then the rise of the Moral Majority is really not a religious revival. It is a movement in disguise—a movement aimed at diminishing the power of the intellectuals in favor of the traditional power of the capitalists. The movement robes itself in religious garb and lays claim to the knowledge of God's will for America.

While I am not an ardent defender of the capitalistic means for dispensing power and status, I do believe it is essential to recognize that the people of ideas—the people who daily excoriate the capitalistic system—are just as hungry for power and status. Like the Moral Majority, they too robe themselves in righteous garb. They are "for people and against the capitalistic system." They are "for self-determination and against capitalistic exploitation." And, in all honesty, they are for their own power and status and against capitalistic power and status.

We need to be certain that all the masks are off. The drive to achieve power and status is present in the lives of all humans. While I personally dislike the selfishness of many supporters of the capitalistic philosophy, there is something to be said for their frankness. They want power and status for themselves. Compare this with those people who, under the banner of religious or humanitarian motives, are just as selfishly seeking power and status for themselves. Are we not all cut from the same cloth?

Addiction to Power

The third and most seductive temptation to which Jesus was subjected in the wilderness was the offer of power. Considering his vital mission on earth, one wonders why he did not succumb to such a temptation, perhaps just a little bit? For us who live in a culture where seemingly nothing can get done without the use of power, it seems incredible that Jesus totally rejected the offer.

Jesus did use power, but it is described as the power flowing from God, not from humans. In Luke 5:17, "The power of the Lord was with him to heal." After Jesus cured a boy in Luke 9, the onlookers "were astonished at the majesty of God."

On the other hand, Jesus bitterly condemned the status people of his day for their misuse of power. In talking about the doctors of the law and the Pharisees who sit in the chair of Moses, he said: "Practice and observe whatever they tell you, but not what they do; for they preach, but do not practice. They bind heavy burdens, hard to bear, and lay them on men's shoulders; but they themselves will not move them with their finger. They do all their deeds to be seen by men" (Matt. 23: 3–5).

Jesus compared the Pharisees to tombs covered with whitewash which look well from the outside, but which are full of dead men's bones and filth. He was bitter about the hypocrisy of the lawyers and Pharisees who went through the motions of paying tithes of mint and dill and cummin, but ignored justice and mercy.

Jesus warned about the doctors of the law who love to walk up and down in long robes receiving respectful greetings in the street; and to have the chief seats in the synagogues and places of honor at feasts. These are the men who eat up the property of widows while they say prayers for appearance'sake (Matt. 23:5–6). He had suggestions for dealing with the issue of status. Sit at the lowest place when you are a guest at a wedding feast, he advised. And when you have a party of your own, don't invite friends or relatives or people of status; invite the poor, the crippled, the lame, and the blind. Can you imagine such a guest list at the White House or at the Congressional Country Club?

The difference between the use of power and the rejection of it is crucial: that power which was bestowed by God was the power of life; the power which was bestowed by human principalities was enslaving. The June 1981 issue of *Nation's Business* featured an article entitled "What Makes Tycoons Tick." The basic factor, according to the article, is power. The article noted that "some top-ranking businessmen are quite frank about their addiction to power." It is easy to get hooked by power and status symbols. The craving for power and status symbols can be so great in large companies that care must be taken to standardize these symbols for people of equal or equivalent rank. Office sizes are specified, including the number of windows, types of draperies, number of chairs, quality of carpets—everything. When I was promoted from an assistant manager to manager, I was told that I would have a new parking spot in the company garage, next to the other managers. When I told the administrative assistant in charge of such things that I didn't want to change, he almost had a heart attack. "You can't do that!" he pleaded. "Why not?" I asked. "Because you'll mess up the whole system," he replied. I kept my old spot. Since then, other assistant managers who have been promoted have done the same.

Our children were very small when I first moved into a management position. During those early months on the job, Judy noticed that I was becoming more impatient with the children. She concluded that I was under more pressure in the new assignment, although I didn't feel it was more stressful. It took more than a year for me to discover what was happening. From 8:00 A.M. to 5:00 P.M. every day people were coming to me for advice and direction. When I gave orders, they were followed without question. The people who worked for me did their best to please me. Yet when I returned home each evening, our children did not treat me the same way. They were more interested in their own exploration of the world than in my advice and direction. When I gave orders to them, I always had to answer the question "Why?" Our children did not sit around thinking of ways to please me.

Why was I impatient with the children? I had become addicted to power in my new job.

We see the addiction to power in businessmen who put all their energies into getting to be president of their company. We see the addiction to power in a woman trying to be elected president of the hospital auxiliary. The lay person who has little power on the job may become an overbearing leader in the church congregation. The politician who has tasted the power of political office may campaign unsuccessfully for reelection time after time. A former boxing champion who misses power may come out of retirement and be humiliated by a younger, stronger fighter.

We all can become addicted to power and status. They can possess us.

Power Corrupts

Lord Acton coined the well-known phrase, "Power tends to corrupt; absolute power corrupts absolutely."

During the summer of 1981, a number of efforts were made by major American firms to take over CONOCO. Fearing what might happen to the top executives if such a takeover succeeded, the board of directors voted to give them some protection. Ralph E. Bailey, CONOCO's chairman, was assured of receiving his annual compensation of $637,716 for eight more years—no matter what happened to the company. Eight other executives would receive their usual salary for three to four years if they were later forced to leave the company. The *Wall Street Journal* (July 9, 1981) quoted a CONOCO employee as saying that the executives had "equipped themselves with golden parachutes." However, Seagram Company, one of the potential buyers, filed suit charging that the CONOCO directors authorized "unconscionable employment contracts" for these executives.

Power corrupts.

We can all recall the instances of the abuse of power in politics and government. Watergate and the fall of Richard Nixon was a case of power running out of control. It need never have happened.

Power is a part of our social fabric. It seems naive to suggest that Christians should avoid positions of power simply because of the corrupting and addictive nature of it. If we are to deal responsibly in this society, it appears we will have to use power.

Working with power is like working with fire. If we do it wisely, it can serve us; if we are not careful, however, it can consume us.

NOTES—CHAPTER 9

1. Peter Berger, "The Class Struggle in American Religion," *The Christian Century* (February 25, 1981).

2. Irving Kristol, *Two Cheers for Capitalism* (New York: Basic Books, 1978), p. 28.

3. Berger, "Class Struggle."

PART FOUR

FACING SOME ISSUES

10

Compromise Is Not a Dirty Word

It was an October afternoon at the Princeton Theological Seminary. I had just completed the first of several lectures which were to be given to a graduate class on the subject of the ministry of the laity in the world. We were in a question-and-answer period.

A hand went up.

"Mr. Diehl, very frankly, I find it incredible that you are standing here claiming to be a Christian and yet are daily compromising in your job in big business."

I had not anticipated a comment quite so hostile as this. Without being able to give much thought to my answer, I said, "I find it incredible to believe that compromise is not a part of being a Christian."

Compromise is not a dirty word in my dictionary. The word has several meanings. In its most common use, it means to settle differences by mutual concessions. We do this all the time.

"Sarah, I want you to be in bed by 8:00 tonight."

"Aw, gee, Mom, I'm reading this good story. Let me stay up until 9:00."

"That's too late, because we have to leave early tomorrow morning and you need your sleep. I'll let you stay up until 8:30."

"Okay, Mom."

Family life would be impossible without compromise, as would business.

"I tell you, $5,000 is the most I will pay."

"I absolutely can't go that low. It's below cost. Look, $5,400 is the best I can do."

"Will you split the difference with me?"

111

"Do I get an order if I do?"

"Yes."

"Okay, then, it's a deal."

When both sides make a concession in order to reach a compromise, each party willingly modifies an earlier position. Presumably, each side has concluded that the benefits of arriving at a compromise outweigh the benefits of standing by an earlier position. In short, their positions were negotiable.

Christians compromise in this manner all the time. I'm sure the Princeton student was not alluding to this type of compromise when he challenged me. Implicit in his challenge was an assumption that everyone has or should have certain absolute values which are non-negotiable. He also had to assume that *his* absolute values should be *my* absolute values, and that in my work, I could not possibly function to maintain his absolute values. Well, those were a lot of assumptions he made and I wish, in retrospect, I could have dealt with them.

The word *compromise* can also mean to make liable to danger, suspicion, or scandal. If I constantly associate with criminals, I am compromising my own honesty. It does not mean that I too am a criminal, but the danger of my becoming one is there, and the public suspicion that I may be one is there too.

If this is the sense in which the student used the word compromise, my answer would still have held. It is part of being a Christian to be in situations of danger and in situations where others may come to erroneous conclusions about us. Jesus certainly compromised in this way when he openly associated with tax collectors and sinners.

What I suspect the Princeton student really had in mind was a third definition of compromise, that is, to make a dishonorable or shameful concession. I believe he, along with many others, felt that no one could survive in business without making dishonorable or shameful concessions.

When is a concession dishonorable or shameful? I suppose if one surrenders on an absolute moral or religious principle, it is dishonorable. But who defines the absolutes and what happens when, in a given situation, the adhering to one absolute involves the surrender of another?

In Jesus' time, there was a religious absolute against harvesting on

the Sabbath. When his disciples plucked some ears of corn as they
were walking through a field on the Sabbath, the Pharisees criticized
Jesus. He defended their action by saying that the Sabbath was made
for man and not man for the Sabbath (Mark 2:23–28). I'm sure the
Pharisees were convinced that Jesus was compromising on an
absolute.

On another Sabbath, in a synagogue, he put the problem of conflicting absolutes to them. Pointing to a man with a withered arm, he said
to the Pharisees, "Is it lawful on the sabbath to do good or to do
harm, to save life or to kill?" (Mark 3:4). Which absolutes prevailed—those dealing with respect for the Sabbath or those dealing
with respect for life? Jesus chose to heal and, again, compromised the
Sabbath law.

Paul constantly struggled with religious absolutes. He fought long
and hard to persuade the Christian leaders in Jerusalem that Gentiles
did not have to come under Jewish law before they could become
Christians. He gave advice to the early church on the matter of eating
food previously offered to idols.

Paul's general advice on religious absolutes bears reading by all of
us. He wrote: "All of us possess knowledge. 'Knowledge' puffs up,
but love builds up. If anyone imagines that he knows something, he
does not yet know as he ought to know. But if one loves God, one is
known by him" (1 Cor. 8:1–3).

So it is with us. If we accept one absolute—the love of God—then
are there any others on which we will *never* compromise?

Can anyone who saw the movie "The Cruel Sea" ever forget the
terrible dilemma facing the destroyer commander? A German sub-
marine had just torpedoed a ship, and as he arrived to rescue the
survivors floating in the cold North Atlantic waters, he discovered
that the U-boat was lying submerged just underneath them. If he used
depth charges, he would undoubtedly kill most of the survivors. If he
did not, his own vessel would likely be torpedoed or, at best, the
U-boat would escape to destroy other ships. What should he do?

If it were certain that the only way to save a life was to tell a lie,
would any of us not compromise our absolute value of being truthful?
Søren Kierkegaard insisted that Christianity is not a doctrine. It is not
the belief in a set of rules or propositions. He argued that faith

depends on an existential choice. In the context of each situation, the Christian must decide how the love of God can best be brought to bear.

Without getting into the whole debate about situation ethics,[1] it needs to be pointed out that we are not suggesting that Christians should have no values or absolutes. We Christians should and must. As a matter of fact, until one has a strong moral code, one cannot deal with existential decision-making. The Christian must enter every decision-making situation fully equipped with a code of religious and moral absolutes which will serve as a guide for the analysis of the problem. But at the same time, the Christian must be prepared to put aside any of these absolutes in an extreme situation, if that appears to be the only way that God's love can best be fulfilled.

An analogy in a nonethical situation would be this: anyone who follows football knows that if it is fourth down and twenty-five yards to go with the ball on your own ten-yard line, you *always* punt. Always? Always! No exceptions? Well, once or twice I have seen an audacious team throw a pass and make a first down. But it was because the other team was so obviously unprepared for it or because the scoreboard was ticking off the last few seconds of the game that the unwritten rule was broken. But that did not mean that the wisdom of that rule was forever erased from the guidelines of that team. It did not mean that from that time forward they would forever huddle to debate what they should do on fourth down with long yardage on their own ten-yard line. Not at all. They would continue to follow the rule which applied to such situations: always punt the ball.

We need to remind ourselves that we are God's priests—his agents for love and justice in the world. That means we must not let moral or religious rules frustrate God's action in a given situation. Jesus did not. Dietrich Bonhoeffer once wrote, "Principles are only tools in God's hands, soon to be thrown away as unserviceable."[2]

Compromise, no matter how it is defined, *is* a part of being a Christian. Compromise explains how we can be in the world but not of it. Do we compromise with the principalities and powers which seek to dominate us? You bet we do!

We compromise with the power of a competitive society. Competition is a part of our culture; we cannot escape it. We can support the good elements of competition to encourage growth in life, quality of work, and the development of people's potential. But with an awareness of the demonic nature of competition, we carefully limit our involvement in order to avoid its evils and its desire to possess us.

We compromise with the principality of our occupation. In a world as complex and interrelated as ours, we recognize that we serve God and our neighbor through the work we do—be it mother, father, student, in business, or as a volunteer. While we carry out our work to the glory of God and in service to his creation, we are mindful that our occupations have the power to enslave us.

We compromise as we participate in all of the other organizations of society. While we recognize their power to dominate our lives, we also know that it is through these orders of creation that God can bring love and justice into our world.

We recognize that all people need a degree of security in their lives. But knowing that the power of security can also possess us, we compromise with this force as we limit our attachment to it.

We understand that many of us will find ourselves in positions where we exercise power over people or systems. We use this power frugally and in service to others, all the time knowing that we can easily become addicted to it.

The reason we can compromise with all of the principalities and powers of this world is because we have been set free in Christ. If we understand, trust, and live the gospel, then the powers shall have no dominion over us. We are modest in our personal expectations, but confident that the power of the Holy Spirit can work through us.

Therefore we pray in the well-known words of Reinhold Niebuhr: "Oh God, give us serenity to accept what cannot be changed; courage to change what should be changed; and wisdom to distinguish the one from the other."

NOTES—CHAPTER 10

1. See Joseph Fletcher, *Situation Ethics* (Philadelphia: Westminster Press, 1964). See also Harvey Cox, ed., *The Situation Ethics Debate* (Philadelphia: Westminster Press, 1968).
2. Dietrich Bonhoeffer, *Ethics* (New York: Macmillan, 1955).

11

Life Style

The place is the posh grand ballroom of the Waldorf Astoria in New York. The event is the annual dinner of a prominent ecumenical religious organization.

I have attended many elegant dinners in this sumptuous place, but none that charged $175 per ticket.

The outer room is crowded with people who have just come through a long receiving line and are standing three deep around several bars, waiting to put down $3.60 each for their favorite scotch or bourbon drink. At one end of the room is a punch bowl where nonalcoholic refreshments are offered free. The bars are busier.

Beautifully dressed people are greeting each other with hugs and handshakes. Evening gowns and black ties are everywhere. I feel underdressed in my blue pinstripe, but am consoled by the fact that most of the clergy are also here in their business uniforms. As I look around the room, I wonder how many really paid $175 to get in, and how many are guests, as am I.

When it is time for dinner, the overhead lights flash and the one thousand guests begin making their way into the grand ballroom. The tables are lovely; each has a centerpiece of red and white carnations flanked by two candles on a crisp powder-blue table cloth. There is polite applause as the featured speakers and important guests make their way to the huge dais on the stage.

The evening begins with the singing of the "Star Spangled Banner," followed by a short invocation. I feel uneasy. The last time I was in this room was for a banquet of the American Iron and Steel Institute. Their program opened exactly the same way. Is this event any different because of its religious nature?

We are all seated, and then begin the introductions of the other seven people at our table. One man is a college president, with his

116

wife. Another is an advertising executive. On my left is a clergyman from New York. To my right is a young black man who immediately introduces me to his boss. They are with the J. P. Stevens Company, and the young man explains that he is in a department for urban affairs. I express interest in his job, considering the long struggle black workers have been having in the South to organize unions in the J. P. Stevens plants. He explains that it is his assignment to try to keep things calm in those communities where feelings are running high. "And he's a hell of a good peacemaker," his elderly white boss adds as he slaps him on the back. The handsome young black man smiles, but his eyes are not happy. I feel sad.

Following the Baked Alaska, the toastmaster introduces the thirty honored guests on the dais. He then reviews for us the activities of the past year and shows huge slides of some of the current programs of the organization. They are slick. The audience applauds in appreciation.

Next comes an entertainer who tells a long series of ethnic jokes. This is a religious organization? I can't believe it. But he says it is all okay because he has an ethnic joke for every possible group. He is right; no one escapes. That makes it fair. When he tells the one about the black man who arrives at the pearly gates after marrying a white woman on the steps of a courthouse in Mississippi, my young dinner companion from J. P. Stevens roars with laughter. It is the thing to do.

An annual award is made to an outstanding humanitarian, an acceptance speech is made, and pictures are taken. The program ends with a benediction and the singing of "This Is My Country."

We all say good night and make our way to the doors. As I emerge from the Waldorf and walk north on glittering Park Avenue, I feel troubled. Is this what religion in America is all about? The evening program was just like any other trade association meeting I've attended at the Waldorf, except it was a bit more lavish. The reception, the cocktails, the dinner, the speeches, the jokes, even the music was a carbon copy of every business affair I've been a part of at that hotel. What was the point of such an elegant dinner? Is this the life style for Christians in the twentieth century?

Lancaster

It is Saturday morning, and I am on the highway from Reading to Lancaster. I come over a rise in the road and suddenly have to put on the brakes. Ahead of me is an enclosed buggy being pulled by a single horse. It is completely black except for an orange reflective triangle fastened to the back frame. It is an Amish family on the way to market.

We poke along at about fifteen miles an hour behind the buggy. Traffic quickly builds up behind us. But the buggy stays on the highway with the driver apparently totally indifferent to the long line of cars impatiently crawling behind.

When I come to a passing zone, I swing around the buggy and, as I come alongside it, I look to see who is in it. Driving the buggy is a father with a long black beard and a broad-brimmed hat. The mother sits next to him, and two children are in a back seat. All are dressed totally in black. As I pass, I wave to them. They look straight ahead, indifferent to my greeting.

What an interesting group of people the Amish are. Tracing their ancestry back to the Anabaptist persecutions of sixteenth-century Europe, this strain of the Mennonite movement has refused to accept the life style of contemporary America. Out of religious conviction, they have stuck to their image of the "plain people." The men wear broad-brimmed hats, beards, and home-made clothes fastened with hooks and eyes instead of buttons. The women wear long, brightly-colored dresses with black capes over the shoulders, large bonnets, and black shoes and stockings. Although the Amish farmers are quite productive, they shun the use of modern farm equipment. They do not drive automobiles. Their homes are without electric lights, central heating, indoor plumbing, or telephones. They worship in their Pennsylvania Dutch tongue.

Their philosophy of community runs counter to that of the rest of American society in a number of ways. The Amish do not believe in insurance or social security; they take care of their own. They frequently are in conflict with state government over the issue of sending their children through public high school. Only a very basic education is needed for farming. While they live a spartan existence, they are far from gloomy. To talk with them is to recognize a peculiar serenity which also is not typical of the rest of America.

As I continue down the road, I wonder. Has their life style, devoid of electric lights, automobiles, tractors, and telephones brought them closer to God? By rejecting higher education, are they denying their

God-given potential? As they struggle against big government, are they effectively witnessing to their faith? Are they carrying out God's will by refusing to go along with American culture? Is this the life style for Christians in the twentieth century?

What is the life style for Christians in America today? Is it symbolized by the magnificent candelabra of the grand ballroom of the Waldorf Astoria or by the soft glow of kerosene lamps in the simple kitchens of Lancaster County?

As we Christians in twentieth-century America consider our life styles, it is important to remind ourselves that the resources of this planet are limited and that they are far from evenly distributed.

Depletion of Resources

The speed with which the earth has been depleting its own resources was brought sharply into focus in 1972 by the publication of the book, *The Limits to Growth*.[1] Under the auspices of the Club of Rome, an international association of scientists, educators, economists, humanists, industrialists, and civil servants, an ambitious study was begun in 1970 called "The Project on the Predicament of Mankind." The final report on this project was summarized in what has become one of the most provocative books of that decade. The book made headlines all over the world and is still considered a keystone reference in the study of resources.

With the aid of giant computers at MIT, the project team was able to predict at what time certain resources would be depleted, given various assumptions. If the "worst case" assumptions were made, that is, if world population continued to grow at its current exponential rate, if food and certain nonrenewable resources were consumed at their present rates, if the carbon dioxide concentration continued to grow at its existing rate, and so on, the computers forecast there would be global disaster within the next century.

Predictions were made with regard to the depletion of nonrenewable resources. For example, assuming current rates of growth continue, the earth would exhaust all its known reserves of aluminum by about the year 2000, iron by about 2060, coal by about 2070, and petroleum by about 1990.

These predictions have come under attack because they are based: (1) on assuming that consumption will continue to grow as it has, and

(2) on assuming that all of the world's resources are now known. Since 1972, the dramatic increase of petroleum costs has caused a slowdown in the rate of consumption of that resource, but as a consequence, the rate of coal consumption has increased. Obviously, a similar computer study made today would give a later date for oil depletion and an earlier date for coal depletion—assuming no new resources of either have been found, and they have.

Critics of the Club of Rome report argue that in our dynamic and interdependent global society, offsetting events continually occur. The Arabs raise the price of oil and its consumption rate changes. A severe shortage of food in one country will change the population growth rate. But while there are such shortcomings in the study, the basic conclusion remains: we are a finite planet with finite resources.

Colonel Al Worden, one of the astronauts who went to the moon on the Apollo 15 flight, had dinner with us one evening at an industry convention. He said that all the moon astronauts returned with the same profound conviction: the earth is a small, finite ball in a vast universe. It has a limited amount of water and land mass, and thus only a given amount of minerals and energy resources upon which the human race can draw. We must use those resources wisely.

While there is a large body of support for the conservation of our resources, there is at the same time a group of people who put great faith in technology. They point out that technological advances have changed the face of world problems in the past, for example, the "green revolution," and they will continue to do so in the future. The argument goes that as fossil fuels run out, other sources of energy will become available. And by the time all of our aluminum is gone, substitutes will have been discovered.

We need to remember, however, that conservation of resources and technological development are both ideologies. They can serve our needs or they can make us servants of their needs if we let them. There are people today who are so possessed by the ideology of conservation or the ideology of technology that they detract from rather than help in dealing with the issue of life style on a finite planet.

Maldistribution of Resources

Even if we were able to assure ourselves that the earth's resources would not be exhausted, we would still be faced with the problem of a maldistribution of resources. The facts have been presented many times before: the wealthy one-third of the world's population claims eighty-seven percent of the world's Gross National Product. The poor two-thirds is left with thirteen percent. The Club of Rome report indicated that the United States alone currently consumes forty-two percent of the annual world production of aluminum, forty-four percent of the coal, thirty-three percent of the iron, thirty-eight percent of the nickel, and so on. No country in the world consumes a greater share of nonrenewable natural resources than the United States. Our five percent of the world's population earns forty percent of the world's income. At the present American standard of living, the earth could support only five hundred million people instead of the three and one-half billion people currently alive. That our world's wealth is badly distributed is beyond any argument.

On the issue of the morality of maldistribution, a debate arises—in the wealthy countries, one might add—as to whether or not there should be an equal distribution among the people of the world. In the one camp are those who feel that all people of the earth have an equal entitlement to its resources. The fact that an underdeveloped nation is lacking in the technology or geographic location or capacity to secure its share of world resources should not detract from its claim upon them, goes the argument. On the other side of the debate are those who feel that those who procure resources are entitled to use them. "Look," the argument goes, "we grow more food per capita in the USA than any other nation; why shouldn't we eat more?" Or, "If we hadn't dug the cobalt from the mines in Africa, it would still be in the ground." Underlying this philosophy is the notion that maldistribution is really the fault of the "have-nots," and if they would stop crying about it and start working on it, they'd begin to get a larger share of the earth's wealth. If someone really believes this, then they should not oppose the sale of low-priced imports in our country, the expropriation of American-owned mining companies, and the unrestricted flow of immigrants to our shores.

The search for a way to distribute the earth's wealth more equitably introduces a wide range of ideologies. One group will argue that only under socialism—or even communism—can there be a fair allocation of wealth. The capitalistic system by its very nature, they say, assures that some will have more than others. There are a number of organized groups in our country openly working for a socialistic structure. Another popular ideology today claims that big business really is at the heart of all problems of maldistribution. If big business could be more closely controlled or, better still, broken down into many small businesses, there would be greater equality. "Get big business off our backs" was the theme of a Big Business Day organized early in 1981 by a coalition of groups, including some religious organizations.

In his classic book *Small Is Beautiful,* E. F. Schumacher adds another villain to that of bigness. He sees technology as a major impediment of economic justice. Along with a decentralization of big institutions (business, public utilities, farms, etc.) would come the opportunity to apply "alternative" or more simple technologies to get the job done. Schumacher straddles the fence on the capitalism-socialism debate, however. To use his own words, "In small-scale enterprise, private ownership is natural, fruitful and just." In medium-scale enterprise, he feels private ownership is "unnecessary," while in large-scale enterprise it is a "fiction for the purpose of enabling functionless owners to live parasitically on the labor of others."[2]

All of the "systems" approaches toward a better distribution of wealth inevitably involve the control of people by an enlightened leadership. Were that control limited only to the means of production, perhaps I could warm up to it. But to be successful in the distribution of wealth, the system must also ultimately control population, the movement of people, the occupations of people, and their very life styles.

The controlled society is not a bad concept—if I am among those who are in control. But the human spirit rebels against being controlled, as we have seen in Poland in recent months. Does the controlled society result in that life style envisioned by George Orwell in his book *1984?*

Of course, there is the ideology of free enterprise. This concept, operating within a capitalistic economic framework, is probably the most favored ideology among most Americans. One of the classic assumptions of the capitalistic free enterprise system is that the "unseen hand of the market," as Adam Smith put it, ultimately balances everything out for the best. Critics of this system refer to its "trickle down" philosophy—that if a few are able to amass significant wealth, their use of that wealth will benefit the poor either through the economic activity they stimulate or through their benevolence.

Nowhere do any of the classic economic theories operate in pure form, and in no country is wealth equally distributed among all people. The centrally controlled economy does appear to come closest in the objective of distributing wealth, but at the expense of some loss of freedom and initiative.

Another possible approach to a better distribution of the earth's resources involves the voluntary reduction of life style among those who are well off. While this movement is gaining some strength in the United States, it does raise an important issue of cause and effect. Will my eating less food cause someone in a poor country to have more? Will my conservation of energy have any impact on people who have fewer resources than I? It appears that the only practical way to assure a measurable effect is to put aside the money saved by eating less or consuming less and give it to some organization that provides direct assistance in less developed countries. But the likelihood of any significant balancing out of wealth through voluntary limitations on life style is very remote.

Recognizing how easy it is in an affluent society to become addicted to possessions and power, we who profess to be followers of Jesus must constantly keep an eye on our life style.

The Bible and Life Style

It is dusk. I have left the others in the hotel and am making my way down the hill overlooking the Sea of Galilee. Partway down I find a soft spot of grass on which to sit. The sun's rays are still on the Golan Heights across the lake. Down below me the shadows are deepening on the water. It is very quiet. Far in the distance I hear the occasional bark of a dog. That is all.

It was here almost two thousand years ago that he walked. He saw the same sea and the same hills. He walked and talked and healed and taught in this very place.

At one time Jesus said, "It is easier for a camel to go through the eye of a needle than for a rich man to enter the kingdom of God" (Matt. 19:24). Would he say the same thing today? Would he consider all Americans wealthy when compared to the rest of the people of the planet? Is it impossible for us Americans to enter the kingdom of God simply because of our wealth? Are the Amish closer to the kingdom of God than those who attend an ecumenical dinner at the Waldorf Astoria?

My eyes look toward the north. In the distance, I see the region where tradition says he preached the Sermon on the Mount. "Woe to you that are rich, for you have received your consolation. Woe to you that are full now, for you shall hunger" (Luke 6:24, 25). If the World Bank estimate is correct that eight hundred million people do not receive a calorie-adequate diet, would Jesus be pointing at us today? Can we be held responsible for starvation in other countries? Should we be eating less just on principle? He said, "Do not lay up for yourselves treasures on earth" (Matt. 6:19). Shouldn't we put something aside for our needs when we are too old to work? Would Jesus have us give up all security? Could the Amish be right in rejecting social security?

"No one can serve two masters," Jesus said (Matt. 6:24). "You cannot serve God and mammon." Are we serving mammon when we buy luxuries for ourselves? Marxists claim that our capitalistic system is money-centered. Does that mean we who are in it are serving money?

The evening darkness now surrounds me. I can scarcely see the Sea of Galilee below. As I look behind me, the lights of the modern Hotel Golan stand out brightly, and I see a sleek new bus pull into the driveway. I turn my back on the dark lake and climb the hill toward the glittering hotel. It was here where he walked and talked, but the gulf of two thousand years is so real to me.

How does one integrate the words of Jesus into a twentieth-century industrialized technological world of jet planes, computers, and space exploration where poverty, hunger, and sickness still stalk the lives of millions? The Bible does not set out a neat list of rules which will give us a precise guideline for a twentieth-century life style. Certain parts of the Bible actually seem to be contradictory. For example, while the Old Testament comes down hard on the greedy and those who oppose the poor, it also praises a just man of wealth. While Jesus told the wealthy young man to give away all of his riches, he was perfectly content that Zacchaeus should surrender only half of his.

The nontechnological society of two thousand years ago did not have the many complexities of production and distribution of foods and goods which we have today. Life was simpler.

We cannot hold up with certainty the early Christian church as the model for Christian life style today. It is clear that the early Christian believers were living in anticipation of the imminent end of time and the return of Jesus. To conclude that the communal life styles of the Book of Acts should be the blueprints for today's Christians may be faulty.

As twentieth-century Christians search the Scriptures, they emerge with life styles which seem to fall into one of three different categories. The first style of living can be characterized by the viewpoint that wealth and power are inherently unrighteous. The second life style can be described as a philosophy of wealth and power used as an instrument *for* righteousness. Between these two extremes lies a belief that the Christian must live in a world of wealth and power, but not be of that culture. This is the life style of "enough."

The Unrighteousness of Wealth and Power

Some Christians are convinced that the mere possession of wealth and power is against God's will. As biblical evidence for this position, they point to the Old Testament laws which were designed to counter the accumulation of wealth and even provide for its distribution. Sabbatical rules called for not farming or working on the Sabbath Day or in the seventh year. In harvesting, the corners of the field were to be left free for the poor as was that portion of the crop which dropped to the ground. And every fiftieth year was to be a Jubilee Year in which all debts were cancelled, all slaves freed, all land returned to the original owners, and all prisoners released. What a radical economic concept!

These Christians cite Jesus' statements on wealth in the New Testament as evidence of a similar rejection of money and power. But these Christians are not talking about the "love of money" as itself evil; they are talking about the *possession* of money as an evil.

Robert Sabath, a member of Sojourners, the Washington, D.C., group which calls for a "radical discipleship," writes:

If we really had a "right" attitude toward wealth, then we would no longer be wealthy. It is impossible to maintain a supposed "inner freedom" from wealth without some outward, concrete manifestation. . . . Jesus' hard words were not just meant for the Rockefellers among us. . . . In the eyes of most of the world, we as average middle class Americans with our "just comfortable" standard of living, are not just the rich, but

the super-rich of the globe, and everything the Bible says about the rich
applies with full force to us.[3]

Christians who support this view of the Bible tend to renounce
wealth and live among the poor. These Christians take very low-
paying jobs generally in the helping fields of medicine, social work,
teaching, or community development. They may live in Christian
communes where one or two will work for pay in order to support
those working in nonpaying efforts.

While a number of these Christians come from the so-called mainline denominations, a large number come from conservative evangelical communities of faith. The latter stand in sharp contrast to other
evangelicals who see wealth as a reward for Christian faithfulness.
One such group, operating out of Philadelphia, publishes the monthly
magazine entitled *The Other Side*—"a magazine of Christian discipleship."

I have been grateful to the *Sojourners* magazine and to *The Other
Side* for helping me think through some of my decisions in recent
years. I do not always agree with their interpretation of Scripture, and
I frequently disagree with their simplistic application of the Bible to
contemporary problems. But their viewpoint is important to me, and I
admire the way in which they back up their biblical understandings
with their life styles.

These Christians are clear on where they stand. As Sabath says:

> Not only is the Bible extensive in its teaching on wealth and poverty, but
> it is uncomfortably clear and plain. The Bible is clearly and emphatically
> on the side of the poor. We cannot attribute, then, our lack of obedience
> to either ignorance or confusion stemming from sparsity and ambiguity
> of material. Why then the lack of obedience?[4]

The Righteousness of Wealth and Power

"I say you ought to get rich and it is your duty to get rich." So said
Russell H. Conwell, Baptist preacher, in some six thousand presentations of his talk, "Acres of Diamonds." Conwell, who was
originally a lawyer, entered the Baptist ministry in 1879. As pastor of
Philadelphia's Baptist Temple, Conwell traveled around the world
giving lectures on his understanding of the Christian faith and its
relation to wealth. All of the proceeds from his lectures and his book
went to the founding of Temple University. He was generous to the

poor and, when he died, there was no estate other than a modest insurance policy for Mrs. Conwell.

Russell Conwell's philosophy was that money and power should be seized by Christians for doing good. He wrote:

> Money is power and you ought to be reasonably ambitious to have it. You ought because you can do more good with it than you could without it. Money printed your Bible, money built your churches, money sends your missionaries, and money pays your preachers . . . . I say you ought to have money. If you can honestly attain to riches in Philadelphia, it is your Christian and Godly duty to do so. It is an awful mistake of these pious people to think you must be awfully poor to be pious.[5]

Many Christians support the position that money is not an evil thing; it is neutral. The evil which is connected with money, they say, grows out of "the love of it" (1 Timothy 6) or the dishonest acquisition or use of it. They argue that money and the power which goes with it can be used for the work of God.

These Christians point out that the Old Testament condemns the wealthy if their riches are due to the oppression of others and an indifference to the poor. There are numerous instances in the Old Testament where wealth is connected with the obeying of God's laws. Isa. 1:19 is frequently quoted: "If you are willing and obedient, you shall eat the good of the land." Riches were considered a blessing of God.

These Christians point out that Jesus separated having wealth from loving wealth. He ordered the rich young man to sell all he had, give to the poor, and follow him because he saw the attachment this man had for his wealth. He was right; for we are told that the young man"went away sorrowful" (Matt. 19:21, 22).

The parable of the rich man and Lazarus is evidence of Jesus' concern for the use of wealth, these Christians point out. The rich man went to hell not because he was rich, but because his preoccupation with wealth prevented him from even seeing the beggar Lazarus on his own doorstep, much less doing anything for him (Luke 16:19).

A further argument in support of Christians using wealth in service to God is that the "up and out" people need to know the love of Christ as much as do the "down and out" people. The logic goes this way: just as it is necessary to live among the poor to minister to them, so it is necessary to live among the rich to minister to them.

Such a position is typified by Glen Plate, a Christian businessman, in an article entitled "The Secular Bridge." Plate suggests that one's job may be the best bridge between the church and non-Christians. Through association with people in one's occupation, the gospel message can be shared. One of Plate's three recommended principles is:

> Make sure that anything labeled "Christian" with which you are involved is as sharp or sharper than anything sponsored by your company. I know of businessmen who walk out of beautiful offices and immaculate boardrooms into an outreach luncheon held in a dark, cold back room. Then they wonder why non-Christians aren't interested in attending. Remember, God does everything with excellence. Invitations on duplicating paper and cheap meals in back rooms only confirm to non-Christians that the Christain life is not attractive.[6]

Is this the good news we share—that the Christian faith is "attractive" by worldly standards?

I must confess that I feel uncomfortable worshiping among the "attractive and beautiful people" of our society. It is so easy to rationalize our wealth when we pray and worship and study together. I get uncomfortable when the Faith at Work Fellowship of Evangelical Christians from Columbia, Maryland advertises an "unforgettable spiritual experience" at the posh Hamilton Princess Hotel in Bermuda. I know and love a number of people in the Faith at Work movement. They are my friends, and they are earnestly pursuing a "relational" approach to Christianity. But in *Bermuda?* I get uncomfortable when a national religious organization holds an elegant annual dinner in the grand ballroom of one of the most exclusive hotels in New York. I get uncomfortable when a local congregation celebrates its one-hundredth anniversary by having an expensive banquet at the local country club. To which many of my Christian friends reply, "How else can the church relate to the people of power and wealth?"

Another troubling aspect of the life style of wealthy Christians has to do with a theological concept that wealth is a reward from God. When Russell Conwell was asked if he sympathized with the poor, he said that he did. But he added:

> The number of poor who are to be sympathized with is very small. To sympathize with a man whom God has punished for his sins, thus to help him when God would still continue a just punishment, is to do wrong, no doubt about it, and we do that more than we help those who are deserving. While we should sympathize with God's poor, that is, those who

cannot help themselves, let us remember there is not a poor person in the
United States who was not made poor by his own shortcomings or by the
shortcomings of someone else.[7]

That same slant pervades many of the Sunday morning television
sermons. The electronic church proclaims God's financial blessings,
both through the spoken word and the visual images. The singers are
such beautiful people with perfect teeth, perfect skin, perfect hair,
perfect smiles. In their flowing gowns and handsome suits, these
beautiful people sing praises to God by lovely fountains or flowering
trees or verdant forests. "Just believe, and the good life will be
yours," is the constant theme. P.S.: Send money!

In their broadcasts from Tulsa, Oklahoma, Kenneth and Gloria
Copeland manifest an interesting theological understanding of
Christ's death. They claim that in his death we have been given a
"deed" to all the elements of royalty, especially health and wealth.
Cynthia R. Schaible, in an article entitled "The Gospel of the Good
Life," quotes Copeland as writing, "Redemption from the curse of
poverty is part of Jesus' substitutionary work at Calvary. He paid the
price for my prosperity—a heavy price. I will not scorn any part of his
work."[8]

The "born-again" businessmen, whom I run into, frequently echo
this same theme. Because they have turned over their businesses to
Jesus, because they trust fully in him, because they have given all
glory to God, they have been rewarded with success. These men are
good people, and their lives obviously have been changed. But the
conviction that God rewards their faithfulness with business success
is not one I can share with them.

On the one hand, we have a Baptist preacher, Russell Conwell,
saying that "it is your Christian and godly duty" to "attain to riches."
On the other hand, Robert Sabath writes, "The Bible is clearly and
emphatically on the side of the poor." With such divergent opinions
from two people who sincerely desire to do God's will, how can we
begin to sift through what should be our Christian life style for this
time and place?

Ronald Sider adds a dimension to the debate which may be helpful.
He writes:

> God is not partial. He has the same loving concern for each person he has
> created. Precisely for that reason he cares as much for the weak and
> disadvantaged as he does for the strong and fortunate. By contrast with

the way you and I, as well as the comfortable and powerful of every age and society, always act toward the poor, God seems to have an overwhelming bias in favor of the poor. But it is biased only in contrast with our sinful unconcern. . . . God sides with the poor because he disapproves of extremes of wealth and poverty. The God of the Bible is on the side of the poor just because he is *not* biased, for he is a God of impartial justice.[9]

There is, then, a third way of looking at life style.

A Theology of Enough

I am indebted to John Schramm, director of the Holden Village Retreat Center near Chelan, Washington, for an evening forum he led on the biblical concept of enough. He pointed me in a direction which has been most helpful in looking at my own life style.

One of the earliest biblical references to a theology of enough is found in Exodus 16. This is the account of how God gave manna to the Israelites in the wilderness. Each person was instructed to gather as much manna as was needed for that day. Moses instructed the people not to gather any manna for the next day, since it would be provided for each day. But some disobeyed and gathered more than they needed, planning to keep the extra amount for the next day. On the next day, they discovered that this manna had "bred worms and become foul." They had taken more than they needed.

One of the Old Testament wisdom writings says: "Remove far from me falsehood and lying; give me neither poverty nor riches; feed me with the food that is needful for me, lest I be full, and deny thee, and say, 'Who is the Lord?' or lest I be poor, and steal, and profane the name of my God" (Prov. 30:8-9).

There are a number of Old Testament instructions on not collecting interest on money that is loaned to someone else (See Exod. 22:25). Why? If I have money enough to lend to someone else, then I already have enough. Why should I exact interest from my brother or sister who does not have enough?

In his book *Enough Is Enough,* John V. Taylor reports on how the church interpreted the law on interest down through the ages. He writes:

It is interesting to see how seriously the church took these prohibitions on interest, and the significance of this fact cannot be lost. At the Council of Arles in 314 and again at the famous Council of Nicea in 325, all clerics were forbidden to take interest on loans, and the later councils at Carthage in 348 and at Aix in 789 objected even to laymen charging interest. The third Lateran Council in 1179 and the Second Council of Lyons in 1274 formally condemned all interest on loans. It was in order to get around this prohibition that Western monarchs ironically invited Jews into their countries to be the money-lenders, giving them virtually no opportunities to be anything else! . . . Even after the Reformation, Luther and Zwingli and the Anglican divines throughout the 16th century condemned the charging of interest on loans, though in 1571 the *civil* law in England provided for moderate charges of interest to be made. Even as late as 1634, the Irish church included in its canons the proviso that the person who charged interest on his loan, like the adulterer, should be subjected to ecclesiastical discipline.[10]

When one thinks about it, there is logic behind Exodus's prohibition on collecting interest.

Leviticus 25 contains many admonitions related to the philosophy of enough. Just as six days were enough for work and the seventh was a Sabbath, so also it was that every seventh year the land was allowed to rest.

Paul expresses his thoughts on "enough" in a letter to the church at Corinth. He writes, "For if the readiness is there, it is acceptable according to what a man has, not according to what he has not. There is no question of relieving others at the cost of hardship to yourselves; it is a question of equality. At the moment your surplus meets their need, but one day your need may be met from their surplus. The aim is equality; as Scripture has it, 'He who gathered much had nothing over, and he who gathered little had no lack.'" Paul's reference, of course, is the story of the providing of manna (see 2 Cor. 8:12–15).

How might the theology of enough govern our life style today? How would this concept fit with the biblical images of being "in but not of," of being strangers and sojourners, of being priests, of being free? Can we look upon wealth and power as our servants instead of our masters? Can we live with only enough wealth and enough power to fulfill our priestly callings?

If we affirm that God is concerned about all of his creation, then there is no area of society where the priestly role is not needed. If God cares about justice, then there need to be Christians carrying out their priestly roles in the political, economic, and social structures of our society. If God cares about the sick and infirm, then there need to be Christians working in the field of health care. God's concern for prisoners is expressed through Christians working in the criminal justice system. If God is to come to the aid of the poor, it will be through the efforts of concerned Christians working in the economic, political, and social institutions of our culture.

In these priestly roles, some of us will live and work directly with the poor, the sick, the prisoners, and the widows. That will mean working with and through human service agencies, and that may mean accepting some roles of power. But in order to insure that our society provides adequate human services for the poor and disadvantaged, some of us will have to work with the institutions which make our society function. That means we will have to work with politicians, labor leaders, businessmen, educators, bankers, military leaders, and editors.

If we are to follow a theology of enough, it will mean that in whatever capacity we serve, our life style will be a modest one. We will accept and use only enough wealth and power to carry out our mission effectively. Wealth and power will be employed only to the degree they are needed to fulfill our priestly role—never for their own sake.

Such an approach to life style may seem hopelessly idealistic. It certainly is fraught with all kinds of traps for us. How much is enough? Can we really measure the degree of wealth and power we will need? Won't there always be the temptation to rationalize the acceptance of more than we need?

It probably would not be possible to achieve a life style of enough if we try to do it alone. But we are not alone. Christians live in community, and it is at this point that we would want to call upon the help of other Christians in evaluating our use of wealth and power. In Chapter 14, we will talk about Christian support groups of various types. One of the functions of all support groups is to help members in their ministries in the world. It is in this role that our support groups would help us to assess the degree to which we are amassing and using power and wealth.

What all of this means is that we live on the "enough" side of our calling.

If I am an executive in a large corporation, I will recognize that to be effective, I must follow certain (but not all) conventions of the organization, but I will do so with minimum commitments. For example, if my peers live in upper-middle-level housing, I will not choose to live in low-income housing, but I will live at the low end of their range. My car will not be a broken-down jalopy, but it will be on the low side of the range my associates drive. In the political gamesmanship which goes on within all corporations, I will use only enough power to achieve desired results. I will be a competent and effective worker, but at all times I will practice great restraint in my use of wealth and power.

Adopting a life style based on the theology of enough does begin to deal with the need to conserve resources and see that they are more equitably distributed. It also gets us out of the cause-and-effect type of thinking. We do not live a life style of enough *so that* others may have more; that may be a by-product of it. Rather, we live a life style of enough simply because it is the proper one for the Christian—even if our resources were unlimited.

By living the life style of enough, we are making a witness to our own faith and challenging the principalities and powers of wealth and security. One who is constantly living at the low end of the range of his or her associates is constantly challenging their life style. If I can operate effectively, living well below the average of my peers, then it would appear that the average is too high. One needs constantly to challenge the conventions and beliefs of one's organization.

Robert R. Lavelle, a Pittsburgh banker and realtor, is one Christian who is living a life style of enough and constantly challenging the conventions of his professional fraternity. Lavelle is devoting his life to helping poor people with their finances and housing. His company, Dwelling House Savings and Loan Association, is a small one by the standards of most savings and loan associations, with less than seven million dollars total assets in 1980. However, Dwelling House Savings and Loan has successfully been making low-interest mortgages and home improvement loans available to poor people who, by the conventional wisdom of the banking fraternity, are not financially worthy of consideration. They are "poor risks."

An obvious question is: If Dwelling House makes high-risk loans at low-interest rates, how does it stay in business? Its own leaflet gives the answer: "Dwelling House makes up the difference in several ways. First, by low operating costs. It operates at only one location; its small office was partitioned from another business." That's living on the low side of the range.

The leaflet continues: "Secondly, Dwelling House avoids default on loans by personal financial counseling. When a borrower falls behind on his or her payments, a Dwelling House staff member meets with the family to discuss the situation. 'We work with them,' explains Executive Vice President Robert Lavelle. 'I spend my evenings and weekends with them trying to build up their confidence.' Patience and education usually make the difference. Many borrowers are behind in their payments, but few ever default on their loans."

Lavelle's company has demonstrated to the banking fraternity that low-interest loans can be made to poor people without undue risk to the lending institution. What is necessary, however, is an operational style that is not typical of most of our banks—spartan offices, low expenses, and a continual counseling effort with the borrower.

Speaking for himself, Lavelle says:

> As an economic person my responsibility is to help others be aware of their economic choices. My business should provide opportunities for poor and black people to control their lives, to make their own choices. I have to give them hope so they can help themselves. To do this, I must get their attention by helping them in their time of need. This means I need to be where needy people are—living among them, working among them, serving them. This is how Christ loved us and is how we must love each other.[11]

Robert Lavelle, Christian banker and realtor, employing enough power and wealth to do his job, living on the low side of his profession, and challenging the conventional wisdom of his peers. Would that there were more of us like him!

Christians who are in business have a vast number of opportunities to challenge the so-called conventional wisdom and life style of our organizations. In my thirty-two years in industry, I have seen many practices which need to be questioned.

The amount of money that goes into the furnishings of offices of many corporate leaders is absolutely obscene. Huge offices—much larger than necessary—are furnished with exquisite antiques or extravagant, modern furniture. They are touched off with luxurious carpeting and expensive pieces of art. Walls may be paneled with costly woods and, of course, there must be a private bathroom complete with tiled shower. Many executives have private dining rooms with exquisite furniture and elegant silverware. For what? To help the executive be more effective? Hardly. It is done to grant status and feed insecure egos. A high achiever does not need an expensive office to prove he or she is effective, and for a low achiever, no amount of fancy furniture will compensate for the lack of skill.

I have seen unconscionable extravagance in the use of expense accounts. Many businessmen throw away their company's money in ways they would never think of if it were their own. Is it indeed necessary to spend $150 for lunch for two at Four Seasons in order to discuss business? An afternoon of golf, followed by an evening of cocktails and dinner, represents a huge expenditure of time and money. I have been part of many such events where business was scarcely discussed. Let's be honest about it; expense accounts and business entertainment are more often than not really perquisites for both buyer and seller so they can live high and have fun at the expense of the system.

How much income does one need? Do top surgeons or bankers or industrialists really need $300,000 or more a year? Do they really need all the fringe benefits which go with those salaries—million-dollar life insurance policies, unlimited expense accounts, cradle-to-grave medical coverage, and fat pension plans? In my career at Bethlehem Steel, I did turn down promotions, but it never occurred to me to turn down a raise. It was always nice to get recognition of your performance through a merit raise. We found ways to use the money, and I guess I rationalized it all because we tithed all of our income. The more I got, the more we could give. In retrospect, I wish I had seen the wisdom of also turning down a raise—not because it could be used for someone else or because I might feel the company needed the money, but simply as a statement that we already had enough.

Our life style says more about our values than any amount of words can. Christians need to study the Scriptures and the very substance of their faith and then make a conscious decision on what will be their

style of living. We may well arrive at different conclusions. But unless
we control our life style, we shall never be free.

NOTES—CHAPTER 11

1. Donella Meadows et.al., *The Limits of Growth* (New York: Universe
Books, 1972).
2. E. F. Schumacher, *Small Is Beautiful* (New York: Harper and Row,
1973), p. 250.
3. Robert Sabath, "The Bible and the Poor," *Sojourners' Supplement*
(January 1977).
4. Ibid.
5. Russell H. Conwell, *Acres of Diamonds* (Old Tappan, N.J.: Fleming H.
Revel, 1960).
6. Glen Plate, "The Secular Bridge," *Worldwide Challenge,* Campus
Crusade for Christ (May 1980).
7. Conwell, *Acres.*
8. Cynthia R. Schaible, "The Gospel of the Good Life," *Eternity Magazine* (February 1981).
9. Ronald Sider, *Rich Christians in an Age of Hunger* (Downers Grove,
Ill.: Inter-Varsity Press, 1977).
10. John V. Taylor, *Enough Is Enough* (Minneapolis: Augsburg, 1977),
p. 58.
11. Robert Lavelle, *The Other Side* (January 1980).

12

Citizenship

It is May 8, 1945. About fifty of us are shuffling through two inches of snow toward a little village church north of Innsbruck, Austria. Our captain suggested that we ought to have some kind of service of thanksgiving because of the end of the war in Europe. Our tanks had raced through the late spring snows of the Bavarian Alps, crushing the last bits of German resistance, and suddenly it is all over. With grease guns and carbines still dangling at our sides, the grimy, unshaven, bone-tired tankers file into the building and slump into the pews.

We sit there in silence for a few minutes. The captain stands up and offers a prayer of thanks for the end of the war, and that we have survived. Again there is silence. We are struggling to convince ourselves that it really is over. After months of fear and exhaustion and death, it is over. We have survived!

Sergeant Hoffman breaks the silence by singing: "My country, 'tis of thee, sweet land of liberty, of thee I sing." Others begin picking up the song, and we stand up. The reality of the situation is just beginning to get through to me. It is over! I am still alive!

"Land where my fathers died, land of the pilgrims' pride, from every mountainside, let freedom ring." For a brief moment, I think of Kenneth and Willard and Frank and John, and that burning town at midnight, and pulling Clayt from that tank with one leg gone. But that is all over. Thank God!

"Let music swell the breeze and ring from all the trees, sweet freedom's song." It's over, I keep reminding myself. Thank God!

For the first time in years, I find myself crying. I am not embarrassed; many of them are crying.

It is January 20, 1973. Thousands of us are huddled around the base of the Washington Monument. A few blocks away, Richard Nixon is being inaugurated for his second term in office. People from all over the nation have come to celebrate that event. But that is not why we are here. We are part of a huge demonstration of protest against the continuation of the Vietnam War.

I look over toward the White House. It is sealed off by a protective wall of buses, parked tightly bumper to bumper. Police are lined up shoulder to shoulder along Constitution Avenue. I see soldiers with rifles. I know that only a few blocks away, out of sight, are combat troops ready to move on a moment's notice.

We are a bedraggled mass of humanity. Most of us are either young or middle-aged. Not many in their 30s or 40s. The smell of marijuana is in the air. The loudspeakers blare a steady stream of rock music and protest speeches. One speaker shouts obscenities to Richard Nixon, and the crowd roars. Men in dungarees slowly make their way through the crowd carefully taking pictures of everyone. We are being recorded. Suddenly, a crowd of young people begin tearing down the flags from the poles surrounding the Washington monument. Some people cheer. I am sad.

A priest is on the platform offering a prayer. Most heads are bowed, but here and there small groups mock the words and shout more obscenities at the police. I look toward the monument. All the flags are down.

And then somewhere in the crowd it begins. Unannounced: "My country, 'tis of thee, sweet land of liberty, of thee I sing."

More voices pick up the song, and before long, it seems like everyone is singing: "My native country thee, land of the noble free, thy name I love."

My mind flashes back to that church in Austria in May of 1945. Then I was supporting our government; now I stand against it. Then I was in uniform; now the uniforms stand against me. What has happened? Have I changed so much? Can the same person support one war and oppose another?

"Let music swell the breeze and ring from all the trees, sweet freedom's song." I look to the White House with its cordon of buses. I look to the rooftops where troops are poised. As I turn my head to the right, I find myself staring into the lens of a 35mm camera not fifteen feet away from me. It clicks. I am recorded.

"Our father's God to thee, author of liberty, to thee we sing."
Tears begin to trickle down my cheeks. This time I am embarrassed,
for I am the only one crying.

What had happened in those twenty-eight years between 1945 and
1973? Had I changed? Had our nation changed? Were the issues
different? Did my Christian faith have anything to do with the events
of either period?

The role of the Christian as citizen has been a difficult one to sort
through in America. The principalities of the church and the state are
constantly competing for our loyalty, and we are caught in the
crossfire. On the one hand, the principality of the state very much
wants to have the unreserved loyalty and support of the church so that
all its civil actions can be blessed by the religious people. On the other
hand, the principality of the church very much wants to shape the
morality and values of the state so that our culture will be in keeping
with "Christian principles."

The demonic side of all this is the reality that if both principalities of
church and state work in collusion, they can get much more than if
they are in tension with each other. And so it is that the United States,
since its very founding, has experienced a love-hate relationship
between the church and the state. Many of the early settlers of this
country came from Europe in search of religious freedom. Our constitution was written in such a way that the state was prohibited from
interfering with or endorsing religious practices in this country.

The relationship between church and state in this country has been
defined as one of "institutional separation" and "functional interaction." As institutions, the state and the church are separate. While
both of them have concern for the general welfare of the people, they
have distinct channels through which such concern is carried out. The
state concerns itself with the maintenance of law and order, and the
promotion of the general welfare of all its citizens through the legislative process. The church concerns itself with the proclamation of
God's Word through worship, preaching, and the sacraments so that
people can live in harmony with God and with each other.

From a functional standpoint, however, church and state interact.
The state acts to preserve religious freedom for all, by maintaining
neutrality amid a religious pluralism and by providing certain benefits
(through tax relief or subsidies) to church-related institutions or pro-

grams in recognition of their contribution to society. The church acts
to support the fabric of the state through intercessory prayer, through
the upholding of a climate of law and order, and through encouragement of responsible citizenship and participation in government service. The problem is that the boundaries between church and state
have become too easily blurred. The two institutions meet in a murky
middle ground which is called civil religion.

Civil Religion

Definitions differ on what is meant by "civil religion." Some will
define it as that faith of secular people who claim no allegiance to one
of the organized religions. The term can also be applied to church-
going people who are convinced that our nation is carrying out the will
of God in history and who, therefore, equate church and state interests. Others maintain that civil religion has come about as a result of
religious pluralism in America. Since so many different religious
groups claim authority from God and yet stand in opposition to each
other, there need to be certain common values, beliefs, and symbols
that can be supported by all Americans. This commonly accepted
group of values, beliefs, and symbols has therefore been called the
essence of civil religion.

I suggest that civil religion is that overlapping area in which church
and state find themselves collaborating on behalf of their own self-
interests. Our coins say, "In God we trust," and when we pledge
allegiance to the flag, we state that we are "one nation, under
God . . . ." Our presidents ask God's assistance in many of their
speeches, and many of our public sporting events begin with the
singing of "God Bless America."

Woven throughout American history has been a thread which
suggests that, one way or another, the United States is especially
favored in God's eyes. That the settlement and expansion of our
country might be a direct plan of our Creator was expressed early in
the life of our nation. John Adams said, "I always consider the
settlement of America with reverence and wonder, as the opening of a
grand scene and design in Providence for the illumination of the
ignorant and the emancipation of the slavish part of mankind all over
the earth."

This theme is repeated from time to time. In the July-August 1845 issue of the *United States Magazine and Democratic Review,* an article proclaimed "our manifest destiny to overspread the continent allotted by Providence for the free development of our multiplying millions." The article was in support of the annexation of Texas, but the slogan "manifest destiny" was used to promote the annexation of the Mexican Territory in 1846–48 and the Oregon Territory in the 1850s. It became a tenet of the Democratic, Whig, and Republican parties. The purchase of Alaska and the annexation of Hawaii were extracontinental expressions of "manifest destiny."

While I do believe it is in order to give thanks to God for the blessings of our land, our freedom, and our government, it is dangerous to link God and country so intimately that allegiance to one involves automatic allegiance to the other. We can say and sing very nice things about our country without linking it all to God's plan. Consider these words on the Statue of Liberty:

. . . Give me your tired, your poor,
Your huddled masses yearning to breathe free,
The wretched refuse of your teeming shore.
Send these, the homeless, tempest-tossed to me.
I lift my lamp beside the golden door.

What finer expression can there be for the ideal of this nation? Yet no reference to God's will is suggested.

The symbols of the state have a way of creeping into our religious life. I feel very uncomfortable hearing the Word of God preached from a pulpit within five feet of the American flag. We can support the order of the state without having the American flag closer to the pulpit than is the cross. If there is good reason for not having the cross or the Star of David in the front of our public assembly halls, our courts, and our legislative chambers, is there not an equally good reason for not having the American flag in the front of our churches? I do not mean to demean the flag; I fought for it, and I give respect to it. But it is strictly a symbol of the state and does not belong in our churches.

One of the most repugnant hymns we sing is "Onward Christian Soldiers." Here is a blatant example of the church adopting symbols of the state to advance its own interests. "Marching as to war," the words go. Well, I've been to war, and it is not as jolly and triumphant as that hymn suggests. Why does the church have to resort to the imagery of wars, armies, and battles—all symbols of the state—to advance the cause of the Prince of Peace?

Because of the efforts of both the church and the state to capture our loyalty, we are caught in a tension between Christian discipleship and Christian citizenship. We recognize our duty to be responsible citizens of our country, to support it, and to work for its betterment. Yet we recognize that our ultimate allegiance belongs to God. As Christians, we are to be involved in matters of the state, but not be owned by the state. We are to be "in but not of." If we can establish that freedom for ourselves, then we can carry out a priestly role within the organizations and structures of the state.

Biblical Perspectives

Perhaps the most frequently cited New Testament text relating to the role of the Christian as a citizen is Romans 13. It is a troubling text for many because it speaks of unquestioned loyalty and obedience to the state. In this letter, Paul writes:

> Let every person be subject to the governing authorities. For there is no authority except from God, and those that exist have been instituted by God. Therefore he who resists the authorities resists what God has appointed, and those who resist will incur judgment. For rulers are not a terror to good conduct, but to bad. Would you have no fear of him who is in authority? Then do what is good, and you will receive his approval, for he is God's servant for your good. But if you do wrong, be afraid, for he does not bear the sword in vain; he is the servant of God to execute his wrath on the wrongdoer. Therefore one must be subject, not only to avoid God's wrath but also for the sake of conscience. For the same reason you also pay taxes, for the authorities are ministers of God, attending to this very thing. Pay all of them their dues, taxes to whom taxes are due, revenue to whom revenue is due, respect to whom respect is due, honor to whom honor is due.

Most Bible scholars agree that we err if we make a general application of Paul's advice in this section. It must be remembered that in his writings Paul is alternatively fulfilling two roles: Paul the theologian and Paul the pastor. When Paul the theologian is speaking, he is telling the people who Christ is. His proclamation of Christ is timeless—it is for us as well as the early churches. But large parts of his letters contain advice from Paul the pastor. He expresses concern about the practices, actions, and problems of the young churches. Much of his advice was based on an expectation of an imminent return of the Christ—as in his advice for people not to marry in 1 Cor. 7:1. This concern for the timing is actually stated in Rom. 13:11 where he writes: "Besides this you know what hour it is, how it is full time now for you to wake from sleep. For salvation is nearer to us now than when we first believed; the night is far gone, the day is at hand." That is Paul the pastor speaking.

Much of Paul's pastoral advice was based on strategy for spreading the gospel. Paul found the order of the Roman influence more of a help than a hindrance to the advancement of the gospel. More than once he relied upon his Roman citizenship to protect his own interests. Moreover, it was important that the young Christian movement not be associated with the political zealots who were trying to overthrow Roman rule and achieve independence. Paul needed to keep distance between them. It was for some very good, practical reasons that Paul advised the Christians in Rome to give total obedience to the political authorities. It is pastoral advice, not theology. Paul's theology, to the contrary, states that in Christ we are all *free*. In Gal. 5:1, he says, "For freedom Christ has set us free; stand fast therefore, and do not submit again to a yoke of slavery."

It was probably *because* of Paul's theology (that all believers are free in Christ) that he felt compelled to give the pastoral advice he did to the church in Rome. At that time, the Roman legions were in complete control of the Western world, and Rome's authority over all its people was overwhelming. Under these circumstances, why would Paul have to give such advice to a tiny group of Christians *unless* some new vision of who they were had captivated them? The new vision was that, in Christ, they were indeed the freest of all peoples, subject to none. They were not even subject to the principalities and powers of mighty Rome. That conviction was revolutionary and, in the hands of children in the faith, it could have led to unwarranted suicides in anti-Roman uprisings. So for that time and place, Paul's pastoral advice was to respect the authority of Rome. It was not a contradiction of his theology. Roman Christians were indeed free, but in that freedom was responsibility and, in this case, the responsibility involved obedience to the state.

When Rom. 13:1–6 is viewed in the light of Paul's pastoral advice for a particular time and place, it cannot be used as a general theologi-

144   THANK GOD, IT'S MONDAY!

cal statement applying to all times and places. In particular, it cannot
be used today as a biblical commandment for Christians to endure all
types of tyranny and injustice nor to participate in wars if their
conscience is violated.

Perhaps the most helpful guidance we can turn to for understanding
our allegiance to God and to country is the story of how Christ's
enemies tried to trick him on the issue. The incident is reported in all
three synoptic Gospels (Matt. 22:15–22; Mark 12:13–17; Luke
20:20–26).

It is important to note that the Pharisees, who were strict orthodox
Jews, conspired with some members of Herod's party on a plan to
trap Jesus. These two groups were enemies. The Pharisees claimed
that God was their only king; they sought a theocracy in which God
ruled. On the other hand, the political representatives of the party of
Herod, the king of Galilee, owed all their power and position to the
Roman emperor. So while they opposed each other, they did join in a
conspiracy to trap Jesus.

The means of trapping Jesus was to be over the issue of taxes. Jews
were required to pay Rome several types of taxes, one of which was a
despised poll tax. The Pharisees paid Jesus the perfunctory compli-
ment of calling him an honest man who was not afraid of anyone, and
then asked him if it was permissible to pay taxes to Caesar. If he said
yes, he would be acknowledging the validity of Roman authority and
thus be discrediting himself in the eyes of many of the Jews. If he said
no, he would be subject to arrest by the Roman authorities as being a
seditious person. It seemed to be a sure-fire way to get at Jesus. It is
especially significant that the issue was over allegiance to God and
political authority.

Jesus asked the questioners to show him the money with which the
tax was paid. Some Bible translators simply report that he was given a
silver coin, but the Jerusalem Bible indicates it was a denarius—the
exact amount due for the hated poll tax.

He then asked them whose head and whose inscription was on the
coin. Contrary to our times, when we show the head of past leaders on
our coins, such as Lincoln, Washington, and Kennedy, in those days,
only the head of the *present* ruler appeared on coins. This was a strong
symbol of who was in power, for when leaders changed, the coins
changed.

To Jesus' question there could be only the obvious reply: Caesar's head was on the coin. So Jesus said, "Then pay Caesar what is due Caesar, and pay God what is due God." The King James Version has the familiar translation, "Render therefore unto Caesar the things which are Caesar's; and unto God the things that are God's" (Matt. 22:21).

We need to note that Jesus said a bit more than was asked of him. The question was whether it was permissible for Jews to pay taxes to Caesar. By using the coin, he could have simply said yes it was. But by saying that the Jews should pay to Caesar "what is due Caesar," he broadened the scope to include all the responsibilities due to political leaders. This would include obeying Caesar's laws, registering for Caesar's census, and using Caesar's judicial system to settle civil disputes. (Jews were exempt from serving in Caesar's army.)

But Jesus clearly noted that there were things which were due to God. Caesar did not command total allegiance from the Jewish people. In short, there are limited loyalties to the political rulers.

Although Jesus did state a principle for allegiance to God and responsibility to the state, he did not set down a long list of which was which. It is the responsibility of all of us to decide when obedience to God takes precedence over obedience to the state.

War

One of the most obvious examples of conflicting claims is when the state requires us to engage in warfare. The Old Testament commandment against killing is reaffirmed by Jesus in the Sermon on the Mount and by Paul in his pastoral advice for Christian behavior in Romans 13. Does the prohibition against killing refer only to murder, or does it also extend to the waging of warfare? If it does, is pacifism the only possible position for a Christian? Is this an area where we refuse Caesar's claim upon us and give our allegiance only to God?

The writings of Reinhold Niebuhr on this issue have been of help to me.[1] Initially, Niebuhr was a pacifist and for several years was chairman of the Fellowship of Reconciliation. During the 1930s his views began to change. In 1932, still holding that nonviolent coercion and resistance were preferable to violence, he did allow for violent resistance, provided very strong limits were observed. As World War II neared, Niebuhr's concern about the tyranny developing in Nazi

Germany caused him to argue openly with Christian pacifists. He believed that the coalition of Christian pacifists, pro-Munich British conservatives, and "America First" supporters were actually aiding the spread of Nazi tyranny.

Niebuhr's criticism of the pacifist position was that the pacifist believes that sin can be avoided if one refuses to engage in violence. Niebuhr's theology asserted that sin is universal and cannot be escaped. The pacifist who seeks to prevent violence by refusing to participate in it is guilty of an illusion and an erroneous theology. Niebuhr contended that most pacifists have concentrated on human suffering in war to such an extent that they have ignored the human suffering in tyranny.

The escalation of suffering posed by the possibility of nuclear war has not shaken Niebuhr's position in principle. It does suggest, however, that a considerably higher magnitude of suffering under tyranny must be endured before a violent response is mounted which could lead to nuclear disaster. The pacifist absolute that there should be no response to violence may, however, be an encouragement to that very violence.

There should be no misunderstanding, however. Niebuhr did not look lightly upon violence. He felt that the confrontation of the pacifist position was constantly of service to humankind. He was very critical of the methods of warfare, including the practice of obliteration bombing in the Second World War. He spoke out against the American commitment to "unconditional surrender" and did much to bring about early reconciliation after the war.

According to Niebuhr, all aspects of human suffering must be weighed. Suffering under tyranny must be weighed against suffering which may result from a war to end the tyranny. As the possibility of nuclear war grows, we must become even more cautious in our efforts to eliminate tyranny.

Martin Luther had also concluded that there were times when the Christian should go to war and times when he or she should not. For example, he wrote: "Since wicked people make it necessary for us to check them and to protect the pious, a Christian may go and slay as others do when God and those who are in the place of God call him to do so."[2] On the other hand, Luther also advised: "If you know positively that he [your leader] is wrong, you should fear God rather than men and not fight or serve; for then you cannot have a good conscience before God."[3]

One who has had great influence on Christian ethics in my life is Dietrich Bonhoeffer, the German theologian who was executed in a Nazi concentration camp. Born in 1906, Bonhoeffer studied theology at the universities of Tübingen and Berlin. After serving as an assistant pastor of a German-speaking congregation in Barcelona, he spent a year as an exchange student at Union Theological Seminary in New York. In 1931, he returned to Germany as a lecturer in systematic theology at the University of Berlin.

Bonhoeffer became a leading spokesman for the Confessing Church, which was the center of German Protestant resistance to the Nazi regime. His involvement in the resistance movement deepened to the point where he became a part of the conspiracy to assassinate Adolf Hitler. The plot failed. Bonhoeffer was jailed and later executed April 9, 1945.

It is one of the ironies of my life that, had the 10th Armored Division—of which I was a part—reached the Flossenberg concentration camp about two weeks sooner, Bonhoeffer's life might have been spared, since it appears that the orders to execute him had not come from Berlin until April 5.

As Bonhoeffer was working through his own position on pacifism, he corresponded with Niebuhr. It was Bonhoeffer's desire to study under Gandhi, since he was very much taken by Gandhi's philosophy of nonresistance. Niebuhr advised against such a trip because he felt that Germany under Hitler showed no prospects whatever for politically successful passive resistance.

Bonhoeffer's struggle over the issue of the Christian and war comes out in the following excerpts from one of his writings:

War is nothing other than murder. . . . No Christian can go to war. The argument appears perfectly clear and incisive. And yet it is faulty at the most important point: it is not concrete and as a consequence does not take in the depths of Christian decision. It invokes the commandment not to kill and thinks it thereby has the solution in hand. But here the decisive dilemma is overlooked, the dilemma which becomes clear the instant my [people] are attacked, [the dilemma that] for me the love commandment extends at least as much to the protection of that which is mine as it does to the prohibition against killing the enemy. It would surely be a complete perversion of ethical consciousness were I to mean that it is now my first duty to love the enemy and, in order to do that, sacrifice him who is my neighbor in a concrete sense. The possibility of loving my enemy and my [people] . . . does not exist in a simple way. Rather I stand in the concrete situation of abandoning either my brother or my enemy to destruction. . . .

With that the situation appears clear to me. In such a case there remains for me no longer the choice between good and evil. The decision, as it must be made, will stain me with the world and its laws. I will raise the weapons in the awful knowledge of doing something atrocious, but being unable to do anything else. I will protect my brother, my mother, my [people] and nevertheless know that this can only be done through the shedding of blood.[4]

It was this thought process which led Bonhoeffer, a pacifist, to the point where he agreed to participate in the plot to kill Adolf Hitler on July 20, 1944.

As indicated in the beginning of this chapter, I have found myself supporting our nation in one war and opposing it in another. I must confess that as a teenager I participated in World War II without giving much consideration to the moral principles involved. Somehow most of us just assumed it was the right thing to do. But in looking back on the world situation at that time, and considering the level of destruction imposed on innocent people, I think I would have taken the same action I did had I considered all the moral issues.

During the 1960s I saw my position on the Vietnam War change from one of support to one of opposition. I think our country did become involved in the situation in Southeast Asia with what were basically good intentions. We were naive, ill-informed, and pretentious about our role in the world community. To this day, I cannot say for sure that our first instincts were right or wrong. What is certain to me, however, is that somewhere along the way we got lost.

Some of my friends who were hawks throughout the Vietnam years point to what has happened to that unfortunate country since we pulled out. They ask if I still feel my opposition to that war was right. In terms of strategy, I cannot say. But in terms of "proportionality," I feel we did the right thing.

One of the so-called tests for a just war is the rule of "proportionality." This rule says that the force used to win a war should be limited to what is actually needed, and that the costs of winning it should not exceed the benefits of winning it. For me, the issue of proportionality first became an issue when our government explained that our military forces had to destroy a Vietnam village "in order to save it."

The escalation of the war to such a level started us on a course of letter-writing opposing the government's policies to members of Congress and to the newspapers. We joined a number of groups who were raising the same objections.

As protests against the war increased, the administration increased its resolve. Antiwar demonstrations increased on college campuses; students were arrested. Peace marches were held in many cities. Supporters of the government's position became very upset, and counteraction stiffened.

Judy and I recall watching the televised account of the May Day assault on Washington, D.C., by students from all over the country. Our oldest daughter, Shelley, with friends from the University of Michigan, was assigned the task of stopping traffic on DuPont Circle. We watched the live telecast in horror as police and soldiers battled the students—our children—in the streets of our nation's capital. Shelley was maced while her roommate, Ali, and her brother—our future son-in-law—ended up in a huge makeshift prison at the District of Columbia armory.

Shortly thereafter came the tragic killing of students at Kent State University. That put the issue of proportionality squarely in front of everyone. The question was, "Is winning this war so important that we will sit by and permit American soldiers to kill our own sons and daughters who are demonstrating against our government?"

Judy and I decided that when a country starts shooting its own children, it's time to put our own bodies on the line. So we joined the many marches in Washington, Harrisburg, and even little Allentown. As middleagers began showing up in larger numbers, the viciousness of government reprisals abated. But everywhere we went, there were police with riot gear and the National Guard or army hidden a few blocks away, ready for action.

My Bethlehem Steel associates were aghast to know what we were doing. For them, the issue was whether or not you were loyal to your government. Civil religion was at work.

The vexing aspect of trying to come to grips with the Christian's position on war is that different biblical scholars can come up with entirely different perspectives. In *War: Four Christian Views,*[5] editor Robert G. Clouse calls upon four evangelical Christian scholars to defend their different positions on war: nonresistance, pacifism, the just war, and the preventive war. Each writer is able to present a strong case with ample biblical support.

This suggests that each of us must examine the specifics of any given war situation in the light of our knowledge of the Scriptures and then decide where we will stand. War is an issue on which we do not blindly follow the wishes of the state. Because we are free from the demonic possession of the state, we are free to support or not support its decisions on war.

A Nuclear Holocaust?

The issue of when to support one's country in war and when not to is an extremely complex one. The information we have to work with is never complete and always filled with propaganda. The pressures are strong to go along with the majority. Without a certain knowledge of the outcome and cost, one can never fully assess the matter of proportionality. Seldom are there any black and white choices.

The nuclear arms race of the past three decades has introduced for the first time in history the possibility of the virtual destruction of all life on this planet. While no one wants to have a nuclear war, almost everyone has given up hope that any significant reduction in the level of nuclear arms can be worked out. On top of all the issues involving conventional warfare, we now have superimposed a spectre of possible total destruction of civilization.

The strategy of the nuclear arms race has been that of deterrence. If we are strong enough to destroy the other side, no matter what the circumstances, then the other side will not start a war. So goes the wisdom. However, what evidence is there to suggest that we have been able to change human nature significantly over the centuries? The fact is that there has never been a weapon devised by humans which has not been used ultimately on other humans. Therefore, there is good reason to believe that we will ultimately have a nuclear war. Deterrence is at best a short-range strategy. In the long range, we must either get rid of nuclear weapons or be reconciled to destruction because of them.

The only hope for survival is a world program of nuclear disarmament. Yet the problems involved in bringing about true disarmament are staggering.

Alan Geyer, a long-time proponent of disarmament, has provided a list of reasons why people feel so powerless to do anything. He says that people (1) seem resigned to what appears to be irresistible power of government; (2) perceive an overwhelming technical complexity; (3) are generally nonactivist; (4) are not fully informed because of "security needs"; (5) do not trust what their government does tell them; (6) see little government concern for disarmament; and (7) realize that for all the talk, there has been no substantial progress toward nuclear disarmament.[6]

I believe this issue is the most critical one for involvement of the Christian as citizen. It is incredible that while our so-called right-wing churches are pumping for increased arms levels, the mainline denominations have remained virtually silent on the issue.

Alan Geyer lists three morally imperative functions which Christians as citizens ought to perform in relation to disarmament:

> (1) to generate and sustain the political will to achieve substantial and increasing disarmament; (2) to be adequately informed so that propaganda distortions may be resisted and overcome; and (3) to understand the legitimate security concerns of a people and their governments—which means viewing disarmament as a process which can and must increase real security.[7]

Geyer adds:

> We must not look upon disarmament as just one good cause among many which confront the churches, much less the very low priority it now claims in all our denominational, ecumenical congregational and academic life. Rather, this struggle to beat bombers into plowshares and missiles into pruning hooks—to cultivate creation's fields and fruits for the sustenance and health of God's infinitely precious creatures—this struggle is the great central act of prophetic faith for our time. I do not know how or whether that struggle can be won, but there is surely no good religious excuses for remaining uninvolved in it.[8]

There is reason to be concerned about those pacifist organizations who call themselves "peacemakers" and whose only option is for immediate and total unilateral disarmament of the United States. Anyone who does not support their strategy is, therefore, cast as a warmaker. Not only is their characterization of others unfair, but their strategy has little chance of being carried out, much less being effective. On the other hand, there is reason to be concerned about those whose sole strategy is to maintain a clear superiority of weapons. Anyone who opposes them is labeled a communist sympathizer or a bleeding heart. They too are unfair in their characterizations of others, and they too advocate a strategy which, in an age of missiles and nuclear bombs, is not realistic.

The issue of nuclear war is a dreadfully serious one. It will not be solved by the strategies of total pacifism or total militarism. It will be solved only if we all work together in the difficult middle ground between these two extremes.

It seems to me that we need to start from a position that acknowledges that the overwhelming majority of the people on this earth (1) do not want war, (2) would be happy if there were no nuclear bombs, and (3) need to have a sense of security. We need then to find ways to dismantle the nuclear weaponry of all powers in a manner which assures them that they are not lowering their level of security.

It may very well be that some dramatic first step needs to be taken by the United States to get the process moving. Since the Soviet Union has countered our every move in the build-up of nuclear missiles, can we not test their willingness to de-escalate without compromising our own security? With the huge overkill capacity both sides have it seems that some creative first steps could be taken.

The nuclear arms race is a clear example of a "power" created by humans which has taken on a life of its own and, unless it is stopped, will continue to stumble forward into total catastrophe. If as Christians we are free of the power of nationalism, the fear of death, the fear of controversy, and the fear of all of the powers which try to immobilize us today, we can unseat the demon of nuclear warfare.

People put those missiles there, and people *can* take them away.

NOTES—CHAPTER 12

1. Charles Kegley, ed., *Reinhold Niebuhr: His Religious, Social and Political Thought* (New York: Macmillan, 1961).
2. Edward M. Plass, *What Luther Says: An Anthology*, vol. 3 (St. Louis: Concordia, 1959), p. 1431.

3. Ibid., p. 1432.

4. Dietrich Bonhoeffer, "1929 Barcelona Lecture on Christian Ethics" in Larry Rasmussen, *Dietrich Bonhoeffer: Reality and Resistance* (Nashville: Abingdon Press, 1972), pp. 96–97.

5. Robert G. Clouse, ed., *War: Four Christian Views* (Downers Grove, Ill.: Inter-Varsity Press 1981).

6. Alan Geyer, "Public Opinion and Disarmament: Challenge to the Church," *Center for Theology and Public Policy* (November 1977).

7. Ibid.

8. Ibid.

13

Servanthood

The room is dark, illuminated only by a single light bulb dangling on a cord from the ceiling. The air has that damp and musty feeling of the basement of a deteriorating old building. We are sitting in a circle on some wobbly old wooden chairs. As I look around, I see only one other white face; the rest are black.

It is 1964, and I am attending a meeting in the basement of an old Gothic church building in a ghetto of one of our major cities. A friend and I are there to see how we, in the suburban churches, can help serve the black community in their struggle for equality. Our adult class had been studying the issues of race and poverty, and the two of us had volunteered to go into the ghetto to see what kind of assistance we could give them.

I felt awkward. It was so obvious that in dress, language, standard of living, and outlook there was a great gulf between us. I sensed that they, too, felt awkward about our presence. We didn't belong there, and everyone knew it.

We talked about their needs—for jobs, decent living conditions, good schools, safe passage of their children on the streets—for all the basics that all of us are entitled to in America. As we continued, I began to suggest possible ways in which our church could help. We could ask some of our people to come into the neighborhood to tutor some of the children in math or English or science. We could appeal to some of our congregational "handymen" to help with fix-up, paint-up weekends for some of their homes. We could donate to a food and clothing bank in their church.

There were polite nods to all of these suggestions. Although I tried to be very friendly, there remained a coolness in the room. Finally one of the men spoke

"Mr. Diehl," he said. "I'm not sure I know how to say this."
His head was bowed. There was a long period of silence as all eyes were on him. He began, "You say you are down here from your church to learn about our problems. You say your people want to serve their black brothers and sisters in any way they can. You say you want to work with us in solving our problems."

He stopped again; his head was still bowed. "Mr. Diehl," he said slowly, "you talk about *our* problems. But, Mr. Diehl, *you* are the problem."

I gulped.

"Mr. Diehl," he continued, "I swear to God I don't understand you. You live in the lily-white suburbs and twice a day your commuter train takes you right through this neighborhood on your way to and from your work. Do you ever look outside your window and wonder what's happening to this city?"

I felt my mouth go dry.

"You make good money in your job and you spend it all out there in the suburbs. You make sure your schools are good, but did you ever think why ours aren't? If any of us in this room came into your office tomorrow morning looking for a job, we'd never get past your receptionist."

I saw heads nod.

"Did you notice the garbage in the streets when you came in?" he asked.

I nodded.

"Did you ever wonder why garbage doesn't pile up in front of your office building like that? Did you ever notice that the city trash trucks are at your building every day? Do you know that they come by here only once a week? Do you know that you get better city services than we do, and you don't even *live* here?"

He continued. "Do you know that we pay more for food at our A & P than you do—for the same items? Do you know that I pay more for gasoline than you do? Do you know that if I walk into your bank for a loan tomorrow I won't get one unless I can prove that I have so much money that I don't even *need* a loan?"

Laughter.

"Mr. Diehl," he said, "you and the other white people run this country and this city. You make the rules. Now you come down here and ask how you can help us. I don't know how my brothers and sisters feel, but I don't want your food and clothing. I just wish you'd go away. And if you really do care about us, for God's sake change the rules so we get a break!''

How *do* we carry out Christian servanthood in the twentieth century? Jesus said, "It shall not be so among you; but whoever would be great among you must be your servant, and whoever would be first among you must be your slave; even as the Son of man came not to be served but to serve, and to give his life as a ransom for many" (Matt. 20:26–28). What does that mean in terms of our Christian servanthood? Do we serve when we are among the poor in the heart of the city or when we are in our comfortable suburbs?

John 13 tells of how, on the night in which he was betrayed, Jesus washed the feet of the disciples.

> When he had washed their feet, and taken his garments, and resumed his place, he said to them, "Do you know what I have done to you? You call me Teacher and Lord; and you are right, for so I am. If I then, your Lord and Teacher, have washed your feet, you also ought to wash one another's feet. For I have given you an example, that you also should do as I have done to you. Truly, truly, I say to you, a servant is not greater than his master; nor is he who is sent greater than he who sent him. If you know these things, blessed are you if you do them" (John 13:12–17).

Are we literally to wash the feet of the poor in order to serve them? The man who bitterly criticized me in that dark church basement didn't want his feet washed; he wanted me to do something about the system.

Paul's description of the Christ in his letter to the church at Philippi says, "but emptied himself, taking the form of a servant, being born in the likeness of men" (Phil. 2:7). There is strong indication that Jesus saw servanthood as the actual placing of oneself below the status of the one to be served. Jesus did not use the word *service* to describe actions of people of power and wealth. In fact, before Pilate, he intentionally rendered himself powerless in his own defense. Jesus, the suffering servant, totally abstained from the use of power derived from the political, social, and religious organizations of his time.

Is the Christian style of servanthood in the twentieth century one which has nothing to do with the power structures of our society?

Yes, say many modern Christian radicals. Socially conscious evangelicals are very strong on the point that Christians must identify with the powerless in servanthood and not work with the institutions of power. Jim Wallis, editor of *Sojourners* magazine, writes in his book, *Agenda for a Biblical People:*

> No longer can we avoid what the implications of the servanthood of God in Jesus Christ hold for the political witness of the church. The grasping of the church for political and even military power in an attempt to gain control and influence in its society is a direct contradiction to the way of Christ. When we strive for power on the world's terms, we merely demonstrate our degree of conformity with the systems and ideologies of the world and show our acceptance of their definitions of what is important and what constitutes greatness. The New Testament sees greatness not as the exercise of political authority and military might, but as the willingness to serve others even at great personal cost and sacrifice. Jesus' kingship is exercised as servanthood.[1]

Wallis continues:

> The notion of "Christian responsibility" has suffered much distortion and abuse in recent times. In seeking to be responsible to the world, many have come to accept the world's own assumptions and norms of what responsibility is. The accepted canons of political realism and economic necessity that prevail in the world's ideological systems have increasingly dominated the discussion of what should constitute responsible Christian action in the world. . . . Do our norms for action derive from what the world considers to be helpful, necessary, realistic, relevant and responsible, or do the norms of Christian responsibility derive from the biblical witness, and, most crucially, from the manner of life and death of Jesus Christ in the world?[2]

Wallis poses the dilemma which is at the heart of this chapter: "Our conflict is this: it seems to us impossible to be both what the world's political realities set forth as 'responsible' and to take up the style of the crucified servant which is clearly the manner of the life and death of Jesus Christ as revealed in the New Testament." The choice, therefore, is this:

> The New Testament ethic is based upon obedience and faithfulness, not upon expedience and calculation. We have neither the insight nor the moral right to choose to compromise with evil so that good might result . . . Our part in God's action in history is to be a servant people who

live in radical obedience to Jesus Christ in whom is revealed God's will for human life and society. Faith is the willingness to pursue the seemingly ineffectual path of obedience and trusting God for the results.[3]

Therein lies a dilemma for the contemporary Christian. Can we really say that when the wealthy give to the poor they are "serving them"? Is it truly Christian servanthood when we use our positions of power to change laws in order to benefit the powerless? Is that really the kind of servanthood which Jesus demonstrated?

The magazine, *The Other Side,* consistently raises the same issue. In one of its articles, John G. Alexander writes about "Going to the End of the Line." He points out that the obsession with being successful is one of the driving forces in the world today. He argues that we should follow the life style of Jesus. "He [Jesus] doesn't want us to be struggling to get to the front of the line," writes Alexander. "He wants us to go voluntarily to the back of the line. Like he did."

Stating that a "central theme of the New Testament is that we are to follow Jesus," Alexander asks the appropriate question: "But what does it mean to follow Jesus? Are we to wear sandals, live in Israel, wear robes made out of a single piece of cloth. Or what?" He continues:

> This lack of clarity about what it means to follow Jesus has encouraged a lot of us to neglect the idea. However, the context of the passages telling us to follow Jesus makes the meaning reasonably clear. We are being told to abandon success: our careers, our money, our peers, security, family, reputation. It means leaving everything to become servants who will suffer. It means moving to the back of the line.[4]

To give up all one has is a painful thing to contemplate. Are we rationalizing such a radical step when we continue to ask the question if this is truly the style of servanthood for the twentieth century? Is this style going to change the situation in our ghettos?

Throughout history people have tried to live in the style of Jesus. One of the best examples is Francis Bernardone, who later was known as Saint Francis of Assisi. He was born in 1182 into the family of a wealthy textile merchant. Through a series of visions and mystical experiences, Francis was given to understand that the program of his life was to be the observance of the gospel. The verses in Matthew (Matt. 10:7–13) in which Jesus sends out the disciples on a mission of healing and preaching but without any money or possessions were of profound influence on Francis. Adopting this style of life, he renounced all his wealth and forever after refused ownership of any property.

Francis's preaching initiated a strong penitential movement in Italy, which spread elsewhere among the laity and later developed into the Third Order. According to the rules set down by Francis for his followers, they were to be "strangers and sojourners in this world." They were to use material things but never possess them as their own.

The consuming passion of St. Francis was to achieve a literal imitation of Jesus. Legend has it that he became so Christlike that two years before his death he received the stigmata—the imprints on his hands, feet, side, and back of the wounds endured by Christ.

It is not known to what degree St. Francis felt he was successful in imitating Jesus, but his life has provided an inspiration and vision for thousands of other Christians to follow.

Are the radical Christians right? Is true Christian servanthood found only in the imitation of the life style of Jesus? With all due respect to those dedicated communities of radical Christian discipleship, I think they have drawn too narrow a picture of what was the essential mission of Jesus.

The Mission of Jesus

What was Jesus' mission? Was it to show the world a new pattern for living? Was he, as it were, giving us a revised edition of the Torah? Was he bringing us some new rules for life? If so, then we are indeed to pattern our lives after him, and we will have to say that our acceptability in the eyes of God will be based on how well we succeed in being like Jesus.

On the other hand, was Jesus' mission to bring us the good news that we are God's children, and that in such a relationship alone we have the assurance of God's acceptance of us? In fact, wasn't Jesus by his very life style showing us that we are not to be bound by conventions, codes of behavior, religious rules, or principalities and powers? In order to give us that fantastic good news, did he not have to reject all principalities and powers himself?

Recall how John Howard Yoder pointed out that Jesus refused to be dominated by the principalities and powers. He lived among people a "genuinely free and human existence. . . . Not even to save his own life would he let himself be made a slave of these powers." Yoder, who himself has been a devoted disciple of Christ, says that the mission of Christ was "in this victory over the powers."[5]

It is clear to me that Jesus' mission was not for the purpose of setting down a new code of life styles for all people to follow, but for the purpose of demonstrating how powerful is the freedom of the gospel. Not even the power of death can overcome it. This is not to say that the life style of Jesus cannot offer insights for us. There is much we can learn based on how he lived and the value system he gave us. But the key question for me is whether God calls us to be *like* Jesus or to believe *in* Jesus. After all, if one is to pattern one's life after a perfect model—the God incarnate—when does one know that he or she has done enough to "be like Jesus"? The question dogged Luther for many years.

When Jesus told his disciples that it is much harder for a rich person to enter the kingdom of heaven than for a camel to go through the eye of a needle, they were completely amazed. "Who, then, can be saved?" they asked. To which he responded, "This is impossible for man, but for God everything is possible" (Matt. 19:25–26; Mark 10:26–27; Luke 18:26–27). Man cannot save himself by his riches. Only God can save. By the same token, it follows that man cannot save himself by renouncing his riches. Only God can save.

When that black man in the dingy church basement told me to go out and change the rules so that his people could get a break, he was pointing me toward a Christian servanthood just as legitimate as if he had asked me to surrender all my possessions to the poor and come live with them.

Ambulance Driver or Change Agent?

It is much easier to see Christian servanthood when we are relating on a one-to-one basis with the person in need. It becomes less apparent to us when we go out to try "to change the rules."

There is a story about some people in a small town nestled at the base of a huge mountain. For many years, there were numerous automobile accidents at a particularly sharp bend in the road which crossed the mountain. Because the nearest hospital was miles away, the townspeople decided to organize an emergency ambulance service. They held numerous fund-raising events to buy an ambulance, and the people received training in first aid. Before long, the ambulance service was in full operation, and the volunteers were kept busy dashing up the side of the mountain to come to the aid of injured motorists. Everyone felt good about the service they were rendering. They soon got a write-up in the big city newspaper. As a result of that coverage, they received many letters and some welcome checks. But one of the letters brought them up short. It simply read, "Why don't all of you get after the highway department to do something about that dangerous curve?"

Christian servanthood involves both driving the ambulances and getting after the highway department. The ambulance driver comes face to face with those he or she serves. The advocate with the highway department will never know who has been served.

Judy's involvement in prison ministry evolved from the one style of servanthood to the other. About ten years ago, a friend asked Judy if she would be willing to be a part of a new program which would deal with female juveniles on probation. She agreed and became one of the first members of the Volunteer Friends Program in Lehigh County.

The first young woman assigned to Judy was Sissie, a seventeen-year-old runaway and truant—known in those days as "an incorrigible." For about five years, Sissie moved in and out of our lives as she went from one problem to another. We were special guests at her wedding and were godparents of their first baby. After her husband conned us out of several hundreds of dollars, Sissie departed, and we have not heard from her again. We believe she felt so badly about what her husband did that she didn't have the courage to face us again.

The Volunteer Friends program led to other things for Judy, including visits to the county prison. Her first visit to the women's facility was an eye-opener. Stuck away in a small building adjacent to the main prison was the tiny women's section. It consisted of twelve small cells, each measuring five-by-seven-feet in which was a cot, a small dresser, and a commode. The doors were bars, so it was not possible to have any privacy at all. Outside the cells was a narrow aisle in which mattresses were placed whenever the twelve-person

162

THANK GOD, IT'S MONDAY!

capacity was exceeded. The only common meeting place was a landing partway up the stairs, with a small writing table taking up most of the space.

But the most shocking thing for Judy was the age of the women. "They're only as old as our own daughters!" she gasped that first time she came home.

Most of the women in the prison were there awaiting trial since they could not post bond. Most of them were charged with prostitution. So at any given time, most of the women had not even been tried and certainly they were not dangerous.

They complained to Judy about being hassled by some of the male guards. Even though they had female guards in their section, they were dependent upon the male guards to bring them food and necessities. They always waited too long. By the time the food got to them from the main prison, it was cold. The commodes had to be flushed from a central control spot, and sometimes the male guards didn't attend to that chore more than once a day.

What really got to Judy was the day she showed up to find seventeen young women crammed into the tiny section with the thermometer showing 108 degrees. "There was absolutely no air moving," recalls Judy, "and the metal bars were too hot to touch! The women were cursing and were very upset. It felt like things were about to blow up. It was the only time I was scared to be there."

That was the day Judy moved from "ambulance driving" to working to change the system. Shortly thereafter, a meeting was called by the local prison society to which Judy invited a large number of her friends and acquaintances interested in the justice system. They listened to a woman from the Pennsylvania Program for Female Offenders and then they all toured the women's section of the prison. Out of that meeting came a group commitment to bring about change. They decided to ask various civic and religious groups to join in a coalition to get a new women's section built.

Later, representatives of twenty groups met to form the Citizens' Coalition for a Women's Prison Annex. Among the charter organizations represented were The American Association of University Women, The League of Women Voters, the Allentown Area Lutheran Parish, First Presbyterian Church, Grace Episcopal Church, the AFL-CIO Labor Council, the Business and Professional Women's Club, the Allentown Women's Club, and others. Judy was elected its first and only chairperson.

For years the Coalition worked with people in the judicial system and county government trying to get a commitment of money for a new women's annex. They had many ups and downs. Concern for prisoners is not high on the agenda of society. "The human element seldom enters in when you're dealing with government officials," Judy has often said. "All they care about is keeping taxes down so they can get reelected."

Nor did she get much support from the general public. Most people were unaware of the situation and could not believe that the system was so bad that the women were coming out worse than when they went in. Judy got some nasty flack from a certain group of people who feel that prisons are for punishment and not rehabilitation.

The Coalition got a big assist when the state Department of Labor and Industry made an inspection of the entire prison and cited the county for numerous code violations. Through a series of lawsuits, the court entered the picture and ordered the county to correct the deficiencies. The Coalition now had an opening. Since the county had to spend a major amount of money on the prison anyway, it was logical that they should also deal with the situation at the women's section. But the decision to act kept being postponed.

Judy decided to run for the office of County Commissioner. In her first effort, she failed. Two years later she tried again and, with the support of many workers from the Coalition, Lehigh County responded by electing its first woman to that office. She is now chairperson of the Judicial Liaison/Corrections Committee. In that position, she was able to defend the appropriation for the new women's jail against the continued attacks of those who don't want to "coddle prisoners" or "waste taxpayers' money."

The new women's annex will be completed in 1982, thanks largely to the Christian servanthood of my wife, Judy.

Judy's service to Sissie was on a one-to-one basis. It grew out of Judy's understanding of "I was in prison and you came to me" (Matt. 25:36), which she frequently quotes. She cannot quote a scriptural reference for the seven years of work she gave to bring about change in the system. Yet many young women—unknown to Judy—will be recipients of her servanthood of bringing a bit more decency into what was an inhumane treatment of women.

We must be modest in our use of the term "Christian servant-hood," however. When we work within our social structures to provide for the poor and to erase injustices, we are engaging in what might be called a worldly Christian servanthood. We are not carrying out the role of servants in the scriptural sense. It seems clear that from the perspective of Jesus, servanthood is achieved only when one positions oneself below the person being served. If we feel our calling is to imitate Jesus' style of servanthood, then the radical evangelicals of today are right in renouncing all wealth and power. However, if we feel our calling is "to do justice, and to love kindness, and to walk humbly with your God" (Mic. 6:8), in the freedom of the gospel of Jesus Christ, then we will carry out Christian servanthood by employing worldly tools and influence on behalf of those we serve.

The danger is, of course, that the worldly tools and influence will dominate us rather than serve us. Wealth and power are addictive. It is very easy for a worldly Christian servanthood to become no more than a kind of righteous hobby or part-time penance for those of us who are really hooked by the modern principalities and powers.

How can we be sure we are honest with ourselves? How can we insure that we are using only enough wealth and enough power to carry out our servanthood? How can we be certain that we are living "in but not of" the world of wealth and power? These questions keep returning; it is important to keep them before us at all times.

As mentioned in the chapter on life style, a small support group of Christians can be most helpful in keeping us honest with ourselves. By sharing with some close Christian friends our vision of a worldly Christian servanthood, we can obtain counsel for some difficult decisions and secure an objective appraisal of how we are doing. If we are able to reject the domination of the principalities and powers, as Jesus did, then we have the absolute freedom to be the priests of God *in* this world without being *of* this world.

One such priest was John Woolman. Born in 1720, John Woolman was an American Quaker who became convinced at an early age that the institution of slavery was wrong. He devoted his life to changing the system. From our vantage point in history, it may seem that the institution of slavery was so obviously wrong that it could have easily been challenged. In Woolman's time, however, slavery was a deeply entrenched practice that had the approval of many highly moral people and organizations.

It was Woolman's conviction that the slaveholders suffered as acutely from the dehumanizing system as did the slaves. And so he traveled up and down the East Coast, talking to Quaker slaveholders. Through gentle conversations, he helped them to see the need to renounce slavery. It was not easy because many of the Quakers were affluent and conservative. But one by one Woolman persuaded his fellow Quakers to free their slaves and reject the system.

In 1758, largely as a result of Woolman's friendly persuasion, the Philadelphia Yearly Meeting of Friends voted to free itself from all slaveholding. By 1776, almost one hundred years before the Civil War, no Quakers held slaves. One wonders if there might never have been a Civil War, with its tragic six hundred thousand casualties, if there had been more John Woolmans in our country.

The Christian as servant must constantly be challenging the principalities and powers which oppress and dehumanize people. Wayne Alderson[6] was a manager in an old foundry near Pittsburgh which was on the verge of bankruptcy due to an extended strike. Poor labor-management relationships had poisoned the company. When the problem was dumped in his lap, he challenged the traditional role of management and set out to eliminate the adversary relationship with labor. His approach to labor was met by great suspicion and hostility. But Alderson's sincere concern for each worker came through and trust began to build. Following a settlement of the strike, he was able to develop a true sense of community among labor and management. The foundry experienced a dramatic turn-around and soon was exceeding all previous records for production, sales, and profitability. The success of the company was really a secondary result of his primary objective of developing what Alderson calls "the value of the person." Here was a worldly Christian servant who successfully challenged the conventional thinking on the power of management.

Neither John Woolman nor Wayne Alderson were a part of the system they sought to change. They were in the culture which shaped the institution of slavery and the philosophy of adversarial labor-management relations, but they were not captives of it.

If the Christian in a worldly servanthood is to deal with issues of poverty, injustice, and prejudice, he or she will have to be free enough from the power of the system to look at it objectively, to challenge those practices which hurt people, and to work with worldly tools to effect change.

For the Christian in the twentieth century, there can be two styles of servanthood. One can challenge the principalities and powers by patterning a life style after that of Jesus. This style of servanthood comes closest to the scriptural definition. The other style of servanthood can challenge the principalities and powers by effecting change in them through the use of worldly tools. It may not meet the scriptural definition of servanthood, but it does meet the scriptural definition of priesthood. In a world where people are hurting, the only way God's love can be expressed is through the healing action of his priests who fulfill their worldly servanthood.

NOTES—CHAPTER 13

1. Jim Wallis, *Agenda for a Biblical People* (New York: Harper and Row, 1976).

2. Ibid.

3. Ibid.

4. John F. Alexander, "Going to the End of the Line," *The Other Side* (August 1981).

5. John Howard Yoder, *The Politics of Jesus* (Grand Rapids: Eerdmans, 1972).

6. R. C. Sproul, *Stronger Than Steel* (New York: Harper and Row, 1980).

PART FIVE

THE ROLE OF THE CHURCH

14

Begin Where the People Are

The scene could be at Green Lake, Wisconsin, at Holden Village in Washington, at Kirkridge in Pennsylvania, at Silver Bay in New York, or at any number of retreat centers where we have spent a weekend with lay people, exploring their ministries in life. The pattern is always the same. Initially, we introduce the group to the concept of the ministry of the laity in the world. We show them the scope of their ministry by discussing styles of ministry in the arenas of occupation, family, community, and church. Then a theologian— usually the only ordained person present—gives biblical and theological perspectives for our understanding of a universal priesthood. This is one of the high points for the people. Their many questions and comments invariably suggest that they would like to hear more.

After these two introductory presentations, we break up into groups of about five or six. The assignment? Each person is to give the group his or her answers to three questions: (1) What do you do? (2) What are the decisions and problems you have to face in what you do? (3) How do you see your faith relating to these problems and decisions?

The people are eager to tell others what they do. They are equally willing to share the problems and decisions they face. The stories are of obvious interest to the rest of the group. The first two questions are handled easily.

It is the third question which is difficult: How do you see your faith relating to the problems and decisions you face? It is a difficult question because most people have not given much thought to how their faith relates to specific situations in their lives. It is a question which, very frankly, is not asked within our communities of faith—

our churches. The inability of people within that small group to handle the third question does not embarrass anyone, for all are quick to realize that they share the same difficulty. Group support develops quickly.

For the rest of the weekend, we work with the lay people in a variety of approaches to help them see the specific ways in which they can relate faith to the daily activities of their lives. We try to help them identify their "gifts" or talents, to articulate the basic convictions of their faith, and to bring these elements together in the context of their daily lives. We try to help each individual identify that priesthood which is uniquely his or hers.

For some people, such a weekend has literally changed their lives. Some people have come alive with a fresh vision of their Christian calling, and they can hardly wait to share it with others.

There are certain comments which I know from experience will be expressed by some of the people: "This is the first time I've been to a church event where we've talked about these things," "I've never talked about my job in a church group before," and (referring to the theologian's presentation) "Why haven't I heard this before?"

What we are doing at these conferences is what the professionals call "contextual theologizing." We are inviting people within the context of their own lives to explore what they see God doing or saying.

Several of the stories used in the first chapter of this book are accurate replays of the three-question exercise of our weekend conferences. The first story—of Martin the police polygraph operator— clearly spells out a real dilemma of one of our Christian brothers. In his description of the problem, Martin reveals several issues which, based on his understanding of God (his theology), are important: responsibility to others (but to whom—his superior, the suspect, or his family?), freedom (not wanting to manipulate the suspect into confessing), compassion (being easier with minor offenders and special cases), Christian calling ("As a Christian, I guess I should stay where I am"), and the grace of God (recognizing God's forgiveness).

This is not to say that the theology expressed by lay persons in the context of their real-life situations is the same theology confessed by lay persons on Sunday morning. Quite frequently, there is a difference between the two.

Without any doubt, the biggest gap between our confessed theology of Sunday and our operational theology of the week is that of works righteousness. On Sunday, we say we believe that God's grace alone has made us a whole and accepted person. On Monday, our actions betray a belief that our identity and worth are based entirely on what we do and how well we do it.

The story of Kathy in the first chapter illustrates this point. Her guilt, resentment, and anger are derived from a feeling that she is not *doing* the right thing. While on Sunday she may confess a belief in salvation through God's grace alone, in the context of her weekday situation, she sees salvation only through her actions.

In his book *Called to Holy Worldliness*,[1] Richard Mouw points out that when people talk about God within the context of their lives, they are doing "theology *by* the laity." He writes: "It is not merely being argued that theology *ought* to be contextualized. The contention is that all theology is contextualized." Our theology is shaped and conditioned by our culture, the events of our lives, and the specific situations we face.

Contextual theologizing by lay people—and clergy, I might add—does not necessarily come out consistent with classic Christian dogma. That is all the more reason for its usefulness. We need to resolve the gaps between the way the church proclaims God's action and the way we see God's action in the context of our lives. I am convinced that contextual theology is the means of starting to help lay people make the connection between Sunday and Monday. I am also convinced that the better able one is to integrate one's confessed theology into one's operational theology, the more likely will one be able to "Thank God, it's Monday!"

Conferences and Retreats

From my experience, a weekend conference or retreat is by far the best means of starting the process of relating faith to life. By getting away for forty to forty-eight hours, lay people are able to devote enough time to the study of their own life situations and how their faith can relate to them. These events can be sponsored by a single congregation, a group of them, or a denominational unit, depending upon the specific objectives and resources.

Typically, such conferences last from Friday evening through Sunday lunch or dinner. They seem to work best when people get away to a conference center—or even a motel—where there will be no distractions from home. I know of some congregations that have "in-house" retreats—where people sleep at their homes but spend all the rest of the time, including meals, at their church building. Such conferences reduce expenses considerably, but they do require real discipline on the part of the people, and there is a high risk of distraction. Nevertheless, such conferences are possible.

Lay leadership is much preferred in these conferences for reasons which should be obvious by now. Lay people know lay needs. However, it is essential to have a capable theologian present. It can be a parish pastor, a seminary professor, or a Bible scholar. The theologian's role is to do some teaching, some listening, and some questioning. Many Christian laity are quite weak in their biblical knowledge; the theologian becomes their resource person.

With two lay leaders, preferably one of each sex, and one theologian, the maximum conference size should be limited to about thirty-five people. I prefer to work with a maximum of twenty-five. The idea of limiting participation is contrary to the usual church thinking that the more you get to come out, the more of a success is the event. However, since an objective of the conference is to be very specific in dealing with one's ministry, each person will need some individual attention. That cannot be done with a large group. If the conference is larger than thirty-five, there must be more trained leaders on the staff.

The agenda should be designed to present a good balance of content presentation, small group work, individual meditation, recreation, and group worship. The facilities should be simple but comfortable; the meals should be modest but well prepared.

It is important to build continuity into a weekend retreat. Too many times, people have had "peak experiences" at a conference only to return home without a means of nurturing that experience. Therefore, very close to the end of the conference, perhaps before the closing worship service, there should be about one hour provided for the participants to meet and decide what they will do as a follow-up to the weekend. If they are all from the same parish or the same community, they may elect to meet as a group monthly to continue their pilgrimage of growth. If they have come alone, they may make a commitment to do something to nurture their growth when they return. No one should go away without some vision of what the next steps in the pilgrimage of faith might be.

Much more could be said about conferences and retreats. The purpose here is not to go into great detail about how to plan and execute successful conferences. Much material is already available on this subject. But the importance of a two-day conference as the ideal starting point for one's personal faith–life study cannot be understated.

Christian Support Groups

Once lay people have begun the process of integrating faith and life, it is essential that they be a part of some type of support group. A typical support group consists of anywhere from six to twenty people. It is possible for two people to be support for each other, and it is possible to have a group larger than twenty, but such groups are the exception. The typical support group meets on a regular schedule. We belong to one which meets weekly and to another which meets once a month.

The primary purpose of the Christian support group is to enable members to continue to grow in their faith. This happens in several ways. First, in the environment of a sharing community, the individuals are able to continue their "contextual theologizing," that is, by sharing the experiences and problems of the week with others, they are helped to make connections between their faith and daily life. Moreover, as individual problems are discussed and suggestions for action are offered by the group, a certain accountability is established between the person and the support group. When my support group invests time and interest in one of my problems, I become accountable to them to follow through with some action and then to report back to them.

Second, the support group provides the setting for group study and the discussion of ideas and issues. In our support group, we will frequently read and study a book together, or spend some time on a current issue such as nuclear disarmament.

Finally, the Christian support group provides a community in which the joys and hurts of each member can be shared by all. This cannot happen in a larger congregation. We consider our support groups to be a part of our extended family; they always are invited to important family events of ours such as weddings, special anniversaries, and other celebrations.

Support groups can be organized for specific purposes such as Bible study, prayer, discussion, book study, or special projects such as the sponsorship of a refugee family. The groups can draw from a single congregation or from a community. They can consist of adults only or of total families. Our weekly group is ecumenical. We have a family breakfast every other Sunday morning; on alternate Sunday evenings, the adults only meet for sharing and discussion. On the other hand, our monthly group always meets as families, usually for a Sunday evening supper and fellowship.

Support groups can be formed along professional or occupational lines. A group of doctors may meet every other Wednesday morning for breakfast and discussion of their work. Or a group of people in the same company may meet once a month for lunch to share their work experiences and see how their faith relates to them.

Over the past two years, lay people from our congregation who work for large companies have met at times for lunch with our pastor. Six of us at Bethlehem Steel did this several times. During the lunch, we shared problems of our particular work areas while the pastor listened and played the role of theologian. He was not there to solve our problems; each one of us had to determine our own course of action.

I especially recall one luncheon meeting we had at a corner table of the cafeteria at Bethlehem Steel's research center. We got into the issue of employee work performance. All six of us were in some type of supervisory positions, with one person being responsible for managing a department of one hundred people. There was mutual agreement that different employees had different talents and different degrees of motivation. We recognized that it was totally unrealistic to expect perfect performance from the people within our working units. But we seemed to get stuck over the issue of how much imperfection could be tolerated.

"I guess we all have examples of the Peter Principle, don't we?" I asked. All heads nodded in agreement. "Well, then," I continued, "how do we deal with an employee who has been promoted to a job beyond his or her competency? It is not the employee's fault that management made a mistake in promoting him or her."

"It doesn't matter," said Paul. "If people are not doing the job you've got to be honest with them. If they don't improve, you get rid of them."

"Even if they are trying their best?"

"My department can't function on good intentions," Paul replied. "Performance is what counts. I owe it to the company and to the rest of my people to expect good performance from everyone."

"Well," I asked, "does this conform to our theology?" There was a moment of silence.

"I think so," said Russ. "Look at the parable of the talents. The ones who performed well were rewarded, and the one who did not perform was punished. I think that's pretty clear."

"Then how do you interpret the parable of the laborers in the vineyard?" I asked. "There everybody got the same pay even though some toiled all day in the hot sun and some worked only one hour."

Russ scowled. "I never did understand that one," he sighed.

"It certainly doesn't seem fair," Harry added.

"I think it has to do with the generosity of God," Will said. "All of his children get the same reward."

"Yes," I added, "and don't we confess an understanding of God which says that he loves us based on our relationship with him, not based on how well we perform for him?" All heads nodded in agreement. "So, if God treats us this way, don't we have an obligation to treat his other children in the same manner?"

"We do, at church," Paul quickly replied.

"And in our families," Harry added.

"But how about those we supervise?" I pressed.

"Bill, there is no way you can run a department based on a mushy kind of love," declared Russ. "You just *know* it! You must evaluate performance and reward or remove people based on how well they do. It's that simple."

"In other words, we confess a theology of grace in the church and a theology of good works in the world?" I asked. There was silence.

Someone asked, "Pastor, how do you see it?" Up to this point, the pastor had been silent. He was listening to theology *by* the laity—we had been engaged in contextual theology. The various members of the group had introduced their own theological concepts into the problem at hand—the supervision of poor performers.

When one of us asked the pastor for his thoughts, we turned to theology *for* the laity. Pastor Tom began by giving us his understanding of the parables of the talents and of the laborers in the vineyard. He also spoke of Luther's concept of the two kingdoms and how that related to our understanding of law and gospel. Together we tried to see how such teachings could apply to the problem of dealing with a marginal employee. No list of rules emerged from that support session, but we did leave the luncheon with some new things to think about as each of us faced our supervisory responsibilities.

Over the years, I've tried to bring together groups of lay people to do contextual theologizing (although we sure don't call it that) related to their occupations. I have learned that it takes time and patience for such a group to deal with the purpose of their coming together. Because they are all church people and because of the commonly shared misconception that religion relates to church work, the people invariably move the focus of what is happening in their jobs to what is happening in their congregations. More than once, as I've tried to move the discussion back to jobs, a person has said, "What does this have to do with Christianity?"

I feel strongly that Christian support groups, whether they are organized around congregations, neighborhoods, occupations, companies, or whatever, must begin where the people are. We need to examine the specifics of our own lives and search for what God is doing in them. Since very few people have done contextual theologizing, it takes time to draw them out. That is why the study of a book or a social issue can provide the stimulus for theologizing *by* the laity.

This book can be used for such a study. All of us have had experiences relating to competition, occupation, organizations, security, power, and status. A support group can take any one of these chapters and have each member use the "three-question" technique to get started.

For example, if the section on competition is selected, each person in the group would be asked (1) to describe the various ways in which he or she is involved with or affected by competition, (2) to list the problems encountered or the decisions which they must make which relate to competition, and (3) to explain how they see their faith—their biblical and theological understandings—relating to their problems and decisions in this field.

Similarly, if the chapter on security were selected, each person in the group would be expected (1) to describe the degree to which they do and do not have security in their lives, (2) to identify the problems and decisions they face relating to security, and (3) to explain how their understanding of the Christian faith relates to the problems and decisions of security.

The third question is always the most difficult to deal with; members should not feel guilty or awkward about their inability to make sparkling statements about how they connect faith and life. We struggle together in this area. However, the difficulty with the third question may lead the group to further study of biblical or theological perspectives which relate to the issue.

In Part Four of this book, I revealed my own perspectives on how I deal with the issues of compromise, life style, citizenship, and servanthood. A support group could work their way through the same issues by using the "descriptive-normative-operative" approach. As a first step, each member describes how he or she thinks things really are. The second or normative step requires a vision of the way things should be—based on each individual's understanding of God's will. The third or operative step calls for outlining a way for getting from where we are to where we want to be.

Another means for support groups to develop their theologizing is through the use of journals. Each member of the group agrees to enter into his or her journal the activities of each day along with how faith seems to relate to these events. When the support group meets, members are then expected to share important or difficult entries from the journal with the rest of the group. The group, of course, reflects upon such journal entries and tries to help the writer see the theological implications of them.

Short-Term Programs

For a support group really to be effective, its members must maintain a continuing, open-ended association with it. The better we know each other, the more experiences we have shared together, and the more willing we are to reveal some of our innermost concerns, the more effective will be our support group. Such a relationship does not develop in a matter of a few weeks. It takes months and years. We have had a continuing relationship with our FOCUS Community for twelve years and with our Channel Two group for eight.

Some people are unwilling to commit themselves to a long-term relationship with a support group. Some people have fears about sharing too much of their lives with others. For these people, short-term programs offer a way of doing theology without making a commitment to a support group.

Our congregation has been experimenting with ways of doing theology by the laity within the framework of our adult education program. One of the most successful efforts has been what we call the "Ministry in . . ." series. Several times a year we focus on a particular occupational grouping and give it our attention in a four-week adult study forum and in a Sunday worship service. The forum helps our people understand the dimensions of the ministry of the laity; the service usually represents the first time our people have ever had their specific ministries affirmed by their congregation.

"Ministry in Health Care" was the subject of our first series. We selected this field because the caring occupations are most readily perceived as ministry by lay people. We were able to identify about forty-five people in our congregation who worked in health services: doctors, nurses, pharmacists, a hospital administrator, a member of the regional Health Systems Council, a nursing professor, a couple who operate the hospital food services, and two volunteer ambulance drivers. (Our parish register lists an occupation for everyone in addition to the usual addresses and phone numbers.) A personal letter of invitation went out to these forty-five people, although everyone in the congregation was invited to attend.

On four successive Sundays during our normal period for Christian education, a different member of the group talked to the adult forum about that sector of the health care field in which he or she worked. They were asked to do the "Three questions": describe what they did in their jobs; tell of the problems and decisions which face them; and talk about how they see their faith relating to their work.

Our leadoff speaker was a dearly loved family-practice physician. He told of what he did in a normal day, and then shared some of the difficult problems he has to face. Fred described the way in which he has to counsel with families when a teenage pregnancy has been discovered, or when a dying loved one is on life-support systems and the family must decide to what extent heroic efforts should be continued to sustain life. Our people discussed the issues he raised and examined the theological implications involved.

The next Sunday, a nurse skilled in crisis counseling talked about her ministry in the local hospital. A hospital administrator took over on the third Sunday, and much of the discussion dealt with ways to make hospitals less impersonal in their treatment of people. Finally, a woman who served on the Health Systems Council of Eastern Pennsylvania led a discussion of her efforts to help hold down the costs of health services.

Following the final forum session, our worship gave attention to ministry in the field of health care. During the sermon, our pastor provided some theological connections for some of the difficult issues raised in the series. Then followed a special Order for the Affirmation of Ministries in the Field of Health Care. Those who worked in this field were asked to present themselves at the altar and, in a brief service, they were identified as the members of our congregation who daily ministered to the needs of our community through health care. The rest of the congregation was asked to support these ministers in prayer and encouragement.

Our second round, some six months later, dealt with "Ministry in Education." An elementary school teacher, a high school teacher, a principal, and a member of a school board led these sessions. Again the series concluded with the order for affirming during our worship. We have also had series on "Ministry in Management," "Ministry in Homemaking," and "Ministry in Office Work."

The "Ministry in . . ." series has been the best attended of all our adult education courses. It deals with where our people are in their faith-work struggles. It has helped us to be vastly more supportive of each other in our various ministries. And in due time, everyone in our congregation will have had a public affirmation of his or her ministry in the world.

Our congregation has also experimented with downtown Lenten luncheons. These have been held on six successive Wednesdays during Lent at a center-city restaurant. The meals are simple and quickly served. For the next fifteen minutes, one of the members of the congregation will follow the three-questions format: What do I do? What are the problems and decisions I face? How does my faith relate to it all? Then follow about thirty minutes of discussion on issues which the speaker has surfaced. Our pastor usually attends in the role of a listener and theologian. Mindful of time, we are always in and out in exactly one hour.

Both of these "short programs" do permit people to theologize in the context of their occupations. They provide a small degree of continuing support for those who have volunteered to speak. As I worship on a Sunday morning with those who have shared their struggles to relate faith to life—the divorce lawyer, the labor negotiator, the research physicist—I feel a closer bond with them than I have ever felt before.

I am absolutely convinced that the starting point for equipping the people of God for their Monday ministries in the world is to begin where they are, and then bring in our Christian teachings. It has been said many times before, but it bears repeating: for too long, the institutional churches have been giving answers to questions no one was asking.

NOTES—CHAPTER 14

1. Richard Mouw, *Called to Holy Worldliness* (Philadelphia: Fortress, 1980).

15

Liberating the *Laos*

In the last analysis the Church speaks to and acts upon the world through her laity. Without a dynamic laity conscious of its personal ministry to the world, the Church, in effect, does not speak or act. No amount of social actions by priests and religious leaders can ever be an adequate substitute for enhancing lay responsibility. The absence of lay initiatives can only take us down the road to clericalism. We are deeply concerned that so little energy is devoted to encouraging and arousing lay responsibility for the world. The Church must constantly be reformed, but we fear that the almost obsessive preoccupation with the Church's structure and processes has diverted attention from the essential question: reform for what purpose? It would be one of the great ironies of history if the era of Vatican II which opened the windows of the Church to the world were to close with a Church turned in upon herself.

Such were the words of a small group of members of the Roman Catholic Community of Chicago in issuing their *Chicago Declaration of Christian Concern* in 1977. The forty-six persons who signed the statement created waves throughout their church structure as they called for implementation of the Second Vatican Council's sparkling statement on the role of the Christian laity in the world.[1]

Why has it been necessary for a group of lay people within the Roman Catholic Church to challenge their leaders to implement a statement on the role of the laity in the world which was itself drawn up by those very leaders? What has led a similar group of Lutheran lay people to form a "LAOS in Ministry" movement within a denomination which has consistently proclaimed the universal priesthood of the baptized? What is the problem?

The problem is that the institutional church *is* part of the problem. As pointed out in Chapter 7, the institutional churches—not the church universal, but those religious organizations which have been designed by humans to give order and structure to the church—are themselves principalities, subject to the same fallen nature of all of us. Luther placed the church organizations in his "kingdom of the left" along with all the other institutions of society. Because our church organizations are one of the channels for God's action in the world, we have somehow avoided dealing with those demonic aspects of their structures which, in reality, frustrate God's mission.

It is not productive for the laity to accuse the clergy of being too dominant and controlling. Nor does it help for the clergy to accuse the laity of being too passive and indifferent. While there may be truth in both statements, it seems to me that it is much more productive to examine why it is that those statements can be made. What are the ways in which the institutions, by their very nature, limit and direct the way people act? The reality is that both laity and clergy are held captive by religious principalities which really want to be served by these people. The demonic nature of any organization is to control and possess people, not to free them.

Therefore if the *laos*—which is the Greek word for all the people of God, laity and clergy alike—are to be liberated for ministry in all the world, we must identify and deal with those forces within our religious organizations which thwart the ministry of the laity.

The Separation of Faith and Life

At Bethlehem Steel we used a videotape called "You Are What You Were When" as a part of our training program for young salespeople. The premise of the film is that one's values are largely shaped by the circumstances which existed when we were ten years old. Although we may change intellectually as we grow older, our emotional or "gut" responses to new experiences tend to remain essentially the same as they were when we were young. So goes the thesis, and the film does make a pretty good case for it.

From time to time, I will meet with pastors to discuss ways in which they can equip their lay people for Christian ministry in the world. One of the most common questions I hear from pastors who have the vision of the ministry of all God's people is, "Why can't I motivate my lay people to claim their ministry? They really don't care."

It is difficult for us to understand how pervasive is the dependency role of our lay people. While many of them give intellectual assent to the concept of their ministry in the world, down underneath there is a gut feeling that "it ain't necessarily so."

When I was a youngster, it was quite clear that one's religious life began and ended at the front doors of our church. Oh, yes, there were those children's prayers at bedtime and before big family dinners, but that was pure ritual. It was in the category of brushing your teeth in the morning. My first Christian service was singing in a junior choir (which I hated) and later serving as an acolyte with a big stupid bow tie around my neck.

The adults served God by teaching Sunday school, serving on the vestry, cooking church dinners, being ushers, maintaining the property, or singing in the choir. And there was absolutely no doubt in my ten-year-old mind that the pastor was a Christian of a higher order than the rest of us.

Never in word or deed was I exposed to the suggestion that lay people in my congregation had any kind of call to ministry in occupation, in community, or even in family. Ministry was carried out only within the congregation—and in India.

The Christian "call" meant one thing: you became a pastor. A pastor who left his call "demitted," and it indeed was a disgrace which was discussed in hushed tones when a clergyman returned to being just a layman.

If these impressions of a ten-year-old in the church shaped the values of my generation, it should come as no surprise that we all have trouble relating our 11:00 A.M. Sunday activities to what goes on at 11:00 A.M. Monday.

Our Lutheran Church in America recently adopted a social statement on economic justice. On a number of occasions, I have served as a discussion leader on this topic for adult study groups. The statement is very general and takes a middle-of-the-road position in favoring one economic system over another. But I find that business people and professionals get very upset by the statement. Once the discussions get to the point of expressing gut feelings, the real objection comes out: What business does the church have getting into economics?

Many of our church professionals express dismay that lay people get so upset about social statements of the church. From a theological standpoint, it is clear to the clergy that because God has a concern for all the world, so also must the people of God.

I, too, am impatient with the reactions of my peers in business, but I can understand how it comes about. Let's take a look at it through the eyes of a vice-president of a bank or the manager of a department store chain. These people were raised in a church atmosphere much like mine where all the messages were, "If you want to serve God, serve the church. Become ordained." Having decided to settle for a less noble (in their eyes) career, they nevertheless have continued their relationship with the church. During their adult years, they have, at various times, been asked to serve as ushers, read the lessons at Sunday worship, sing in the choir, perhaps teach a class of kiddies, serve on some committees, and ultimately make it to the church council. Oh, yes, and they were constantly reminded that Christian stewardship meant giving to the church regularly.

In their weekday lives, the bank vice-president and the department store manager have assumed important responsibilities and have their hands full. The former is concerned about having to turn down so many young couples for mortgage loans because the interest rates are simply too high for them to handle. His company has also designated him as its representative to meet with a delegation of poor people who have been accusing the bank of "redlining" their neighborhood— refusing to grant any loans in their area. The situation is becoming nasty, and that upsets him. Finally, he has a nagging concern about the future of the bank itself. Investors are looking elsewhere for higher interest investments. If the drain of resources from the bank continues, there will be serious trouble.

The department store manager has her own problems. Her store, one of a national chain, is not generating the volume of business it did several years ago, due primarily to the opening of a huge new shopping mall only a half-mile away. She has tried all kinds of inducements to reverse the trend, but it continues. With less volume, she has had to lay off some of her employees in order to cut costs and stay in the black. They are good people who have worked hard for her, and it tears her up to have to lay them off. On top of it all, the central office of her chain keeps pointing out that her store is one of the lowest in profit generation and, if it continues, they will have to close it down. That would mean a demotion and transfer to another city for her and her family—which she doesn't want.

Meanwhile the congregation of the banker and manager continues to press them to serve on the evangelism committee or choir or at least be ushers. Both the pastor and the lay vice-president of the church council are convinced that the way to bring new life into the congregation is "to get everyone involved." And so the banker and retailer willingly accept certain responsibilities in their parish because they, too, feel they want to serve their God.

At no time in the career of the vice-president or the manager has there ever been the slightest recognition by their church or pastor that what they are doing in their professional career was in service to God. Most of the people they nodded to on Sunday mornings or sat with in committee meetings didn't even have the faintest idea of what they did for a living. Now along comes their national church and hands them a statement on economic justice, written largely by church professionals and passed in a convention consisting of clergy and "churchy" laity, commending the banker and retailer to the study and implementation of the statement.

Should anyone be surprised that their reaction is: "What the hell is the church doing trying to tell me about economic justice?" and "What does the church know about economics?" and "No church convention speaks for me on economics!" and "The church should mind its own business!"

And what is that business? Why, it's the business of running worship services and Sunday school and keeping people busy with committees and choirs and calling on prospective members. That's the church's business!

The principality of religious organizations, in order to feed its own hungry body, has effectively separated Sunday faith from weekday life for most Christians.

Integrating Faith and Life

What things need to be done to change the situation described in the previous section? First, we need to recognize that whatever we do to equip the Christian laity for their ministries in the world has got to involve our children. They need firsthand evidence that their parents are constantly working at integrating their faith into the real life situations facing the family and its members. That involves conversations among the family which deal with the decisions and problems they are facing and how they see their faith relating to them. It involves family prayer which is particularized—not simply the habitual recitation of table grace.

Within the context of congregational life the children need to see that the ministries of adults in their occupations and other activities beyond the parish walls are affirmed every bit as much as both professional and volunteer work within the congregation. In all aspects of parish activity—worship, education, service, and fellowship—our children need to see that the congregation's focus is on equipping all its members for ministry in the world.

We begin with worship. The liturgical flow as followed in most churches today is ideally suited to communicate the "gathering and scattering" function of the local parish. As we gather, we first confess our failures and mistakes. We receive absolution for these failures and are restored and renewed by the Word and Sacraments. We pray for guidance and support, and then we are sent out into the world in service. The weakest link in this liturgical flow has been the preparation for reentry into the world. Somehow we must find better ways to communicate this final act of the worship service.

More and more congregations are discovering creative ways to affirm the ministries of the laity through orders of recognition or commissioning within the context of the worship service. Some clergy feel the word "commissioning" is too strong, and some feel the word "affirming" is too weak. I leave it to others to resolve the terms. The point is that every congregation has ways of recognizing the ministry of its lay people as they serve the congregation. We "install" church council members and Sunday school teachers in our worship services. We give recognition to the choir in our worship services from time to time. We commission lay visitors for every-member visitation or evangelism calls. Let's find ways to give the same type of public recognition for lay service in the world—in occupation, as volunteers, in family, and in the community.

Some congregations affirm ministry in the workplace by asking everyone to attend Sunday worship on a given day in the clothing or uniforms they will be wearing on Monday. The entire worship service is then built around priesthood through occupation.

Most of our clergy vastly underestimate the tight grip that a works-righteous society has on their people. As a result, too few sermons deal with the liberating good news of the gospel. For people who feel out of control of their lives, who are held captives by the contemporary powers of security, status, and life style and by the contemporary principalities of occupations, institutions, and government, the gospel message is crucial. It cannot be preached too often. The pulpit needs to expose the demonic forces in our society and proclaim the fantastic news that our worth and identity is apart from anything we do and is, in fact, already assured. That is the Word. It needs to be preached.

Participation of the laity in the worship service should be encouraged. We always use lay lectors in our congregation's worship services, and one of the responsibilities of sharing the liturgy with the pastor involves the offering of a prayer written by the lector. The prayers are not slickly written petitions copied from a book of worship, but the honest expressions of thanksgiving and concern coming from the hearts of our people.

We need to be careful, however, that lay participation in the worship service is not held up as *the* ministry of the laity. It is but one of many ministries of the laity. For this reason, I do not agree with the practice of having lay people appear in robes. The liturgical arguments for this practice are not impressive. Once the lay person dons a robe, he or she is different from the rest of the laity in worship. The robe may symbolize more than a difference in function; it can very well symbolize a difference in status. The danger is that the laity will come to see that ministry of the laity in worship is the highest order of their ministry. Why run the risk of communicating this misconception?

The educational ministry of the congregation offers the greatest potential for equipping the laity for their Monday worlds. Education should not be limited to one hour per week on a Sunday morning. Because so many of a congregation's most committed and creative people are occupied with teaching the children, the Sunday morning education hour is perhaps one of the worst times to concentrate on adult education. Evening study programs, support groups, luncheons, breakfast sessions, and discussions in the company lunch rooms offer all kinds of educational possibilities. The weekend retreat is by far one of the most effective settings for adult education. While regional clusters might be responsible for running the specialized equipping retreats, any size congregation can and should conduct more generalized conferences for the adults. Parents of small children should be freed for such weekends through the offer of child care by other members of the congregation.

In our conference work we have discovered that lay people are hungry for help in the "how-to's" of carrying out ministry. Any educational program therefore should offer courses in such skills as how to communicate the faith, how to effect change, how to organize for political action, how to counsel, how to be a better listener, how to be effective in small groups, and a host of others. One course which should be taken by all people is gift identification. We all have certain talents, God-given gifts, which are important to utilize as we minister in the world. Yet many Christians, either out of a sense of modesty or ignorance, are not in touch with their gifts. Courses on how to identify one's gifts are essential as we strive to relate our faith to the Monday world.

Much has been said in the previous chapter about the importance of support groups. While some Christian support groups may not be related to a parish, every congregation should offer a variety of opportunities for members to associate in support groups. The groups can organize around prayer, book study, issue discussion, fellowship, projects, or Bible study. Whatever the focus of the group may be, its purpose is primarily to enable people to share with each other the struggles of life and to support each other in their ministries.

Our congregation uses a large bulletin board as a means of affirming the ministries of our people in the world. Whenever a news item appears involving the work or achievements of any of our members, one of our staff people will clip it from the newspaper and post it on the bulletin board. The annual church directory, which goes into every home in our congregation, lists the occupation of every member in addition to their address and telephone number. This does not mean just "paid" jobs; it includes volunteer work in the community and identification of where a student may be in school.

Some congregations use artwork or signs to convey the ministry of all the people. In one church building I visited, every door leading outside had posted about it the words "Servant's entrance." More frequently will the parish bulletins list the name of the ordained minister with the title "pastor," and then follow up with the identification of all the members as "ministers."

Congregations are using their parish newsletters as a means of identifying what their lay people may be doing in their worldly ministries.

At the beginning of each year, the laity of our congregation are asked to contribute short meditations of their own composition for use in a Lenten devotional booklet. Frequently these meditations draw from the real-life experiences of the people we know and, therefore, they have a special meaning for us.

The congregation in its life of worship, study, service, and fellowship is central in the process of liberating the *laos*.

An issue which the national church bodies will have to face if they are to help their people bridge the Sunday-Monday gap has to do with secular credibility. When our denominations issue statements on social issues or distribute position papers on worldly problems or confront the secular institutions as advocates for the poor and powerless, it is important that they know what they are talking about. The church's role is to be prophetic and, in many instances, that will involve saying things that are critical of our society. Such pronouncements are too easily dismissed by the world if it is apparent that the church's statements are too simplistic or have failed to examine all sides of a given issue.

In the past, social statements, position papers, and advocacy efforts have largely represented the work product of a relatively small group of church professionals—usually clergy within the national offices of our denominations and councils of churches. In too many instances it was obvious to all that the church's statements were based on inadequate study or prejudice of the authors or both. When public pronouncements of the church are so easily discounted, it just serves to reinforce the feeling of the laity that the faith does not relate to daily life.

The problem can easily be corrected by calling upon those with demonstrated expertise in worldly affairs—the laity. No national denomination or council of churches should take a position on a worldly issue without utilizing the resources of its laity and without engaging its laity in debate and review of the issue.

This is not to say that the church's position should represent a consensus of lay opinions on the issue. If such a consensus is clearly at odds with the biblical and theological position of the church, then its prophetic voice of dissent needs to be heard. If such a statement can demonstrate a full knowledge of the problem and a clear theological connection to it, the laity will respect it and be forced to deal with it in their Monday world.

One of the greatest services our national church bodies can provide is to become recognized as responsible sources for the even-handed description of our *problems*. I for one have been bewildered and confused after reading articles pro and con on the Nestlé infant formula issue, on the safety of nuclear power generation, on the boycott of South African goods, and other such problems. The articles are usually so obviously biased that it is impossible to feel that one even has a fair understanding of the problem, much less a handle on the solution.

Could not our national church bodies be the facilitators for bringing together both sides on these controversial issues, for hearing them out, for presenting us with as even-handed analyses of the problems as possible, and for pointing us to those biblical and theological perspectives which seem to relate to the issues? On many complex issues, there may be no clear position for the church to take. The legitimate interests of conflicting groups, the dynamic nature of disputes, and the inability to generalize all may preclude the church from taking a position. So what? Isn't that the way it is for so many of us with our personal problems in the real world?

The Separation of Seminary and Parish

If the local congregation is to be the arena for equipping the laity for ministry on Monday, then it is most important that the professional enablers—the parish clergy—are properly trained for their role. In my opinion our seminaries are also so victimized by their own academic institutionalism that not only are they failing to prepare the clergy for their role of equipping, but they are also supporting a philosophy which depreciates a theology of the laity.

In an article dealing with the separation ot the seminaries and the local church, *The Christian Century*[2] quotes Robert Martin as saying: "The personnel of the seminary—administrators and faculty—really have to evaluate afresh their seriousness about the church, their seriousness about the mission of the church in the world, and their seriousness about the relationship of knowledge to the practice of what they teach as it concerns the hopes and concerns of the culture around them." In the same article Fredrica Thompsett, executive director of the Episcopal Church's Board for Theological Education, is quoted as saying: "Seminaries in North America have undervalued, and refused to publicly acclaim and encourage, the educational responsibilities of parish life." In short, our seminaries are seeing as their end product the academic training of ordained ministers instead of looking beyond and seeing as their ultimate end product the equipping of laity for ministry in the world.

In his book, *A Theology of the Laity,* Hendrick Kraemer points out that Christian theologians, especially since the days of the sixteenth-century Reformation, "have addressed themselves with great zeal and ability to a theological motivation of the training, preparation, function, and status of the Ministry, that is to say, the ordained and consecrated clergy." While the training of the clergy is absolutely essential, Kraemer points out that it represents "exclusive theological attention."[3]

Because contemporary American theology centers on the training and support of the ordained members of the organization, any theology relating to the lesser members—the laity—is considered an *adjunct* to the primary mission of the theologians. Thus, the theologians inadvertently define what a church institution really is—an inward focusing principality which sustains its own life by directing all wisdom and training to those who have committed their lives in professional service to it.

If anyone has the slightest doubt that a theology of the laity is considered adjunct to the training of the clergy, a visit to our theological seminaries will provide irrefutable evidence. Look at the curriculum, talk to the professors, rap with the students. It comes through very clearly.

I shared teaching a course on the ministry of the laity at Princeton a few years ago. It was an optional course in the graduate school, as I think all such courses are. We had some lively discussions and some good times together. But as we progressed, it was very clear to me that what the students were looking for in taking the course was a better understanding of the laity *so that* they could better use them in serving the church institution. And that was all they got out of it. I might just as well have taught a course on how to use audiovisual equipment.

A number of theological seminaries have been trying in recent years to have the laity more involved in their activities both as students and as lecturers. The vast majority of the seminary courses for lay people are ecclesiastical in focus. Their aim is to lead the lay person into a more meaningful church-centered life. And unfortunately, in many cases, the *reason* for offering such courses is to provide more income for the financially strapped seminaries.

The occasional appearance of lay lecturers on some seminary campuses does represent an effort to expose students and faculty to the viewpoint, needs, and concerns of the laity in the world. But by the very nature of the infrequency of such lectures, the after-hours scheduling of them, and the indifference to them of most faculty, there is given to the students a positive reinforcement of the belief that a theology of the laity is adjunct to the central mission of the institution. Not until a theology of the laity in the world is an integral part of required curriculum will students begin to see that their role will be to affirm, equip, and support laity for ministry beyond the four walls of the church.

Kraemer insists that a true theology of the laity will not be possible as long as it is seen as an "appendix to our existing ecclesiologies" instead of an *"organic part"* of a total ecclesiology."[4]

From time to time, the Holy Spirit has broken through the strong walls of institutionalism by means of grass-roots lay movements initiated by the nonordained. In every instance, they have flowered for a brief time and then died. Kraemer attributes their deaths to the abiding conviction of the religious institutions that a theology of the laity is an "appendix." While the churches have given lip service to such movements, the theological leaders have considered such activity as an adjunct—perhaps a welcome adjunct—but nevertheless an adjunct to the nature and mission of the church. Not even Screwtape could design a better way to frustrate the mission of the Church universal: use the Wise Men to maintain a theology which ultimately serves the religious principalities. It is pure diabolical genius.

The Integration of Seminary and Parish

What would our seminaries be like if the institutional church suddenly caught the vision of equipping the *laos* for ministry in the world? They would certainly continue to train our clergy. If I am going to fulfill my role as a priest in my daily life, I will need the help of one skilled in theology, in knowledge of the Bible, in counseling, communications, and in creating an atmosphere in which Christian community can be experienced. My congregation will have to become the place where I become energized for my ministry through worship and prayer, through Word and Sacrament, through adult education, through support groups, and through a constant affirmation of my Christian calling.

I suspect, however, that there would have to be a substantial rethinking of curriculum and philosophy in our seminaries if their mission becomes one of equipping the laity by means of a parish clergy trained for that assignment. A seminary which saw as its end product a laity ministering in the secular institutions of society would want to be doing theology with and for that laity. And that could be very exciting. Imagine the stimulation which would come out of intensive lay-seminary studies on some of the issues and dilemmas facing all of us in this American culture.

What about the matter of living in a competitive society? Is there a contradiction between our biblical concept of stewardship, in which we are to use all our talents to the best of our ability, and Jesus' teaching on servanthood—taking a lesser position?

What about this business of "principalities and powers"? Is it merely a convenient imagery for me to use in this book, or did the early church recognize something we do not? Do we or do we not believe in the demonic power of a suprahuman organization? Are organizations merely the sum total of the people in them, or is there something else present? What do we mean when we rail against the "conscience of a corporation"? Where does that conscience come from?

As we examine our security needs, how do we deal with the teachings of Jesus and Paul? Do they apply to us, or do they not? How are we to deal with the issues of power and status? Does the church *really* mean that we should be like Jesus in renouncing all use of power? Is Abraham Maslow's hierarchy of needs consistent with Christian doctrine or is it not?

How do we address the issue of compromise? What are the Christian absolutes which cannot be compromised under any circumstances? Why do we so often hear simplistic ethics proclaimed from the pulpit?

What is our theology with respect to wealth? How can we possibly continue to read the words of Jesus regarding wealth without very seriously bringing them into the context of our affluent American culture? Is God partial to the poor? How do we minister to the rich?

In all of the history of humankind, people have never failed to use a weapon of warfare. As we head down the road toward a nuclear catastrophe, what course of action does our Christian theology suggest—deterrence, unilateral disarmament, or a blind trust in God? Why is the American church silent on this issue?

How do we resolve the dilemma of servanthood? Can a Christian be a true servant only if he or she assumes an inferior role to those being served?

These and scores of other issues are part of the fabric of our everyday lives. The Christian church must either learn how to theologize on these issues or confess to its state of bankruptcy.

I know many business people who would gladly pay their way to theologize with good biblical scholars on the issue of competition. But they will expect to be taken seriously, not patronized. Similarly, the laity could become very excited about theologizing *with* our scholars on issues of life style, power, compromise, war, and others.

If the institutional church could come to see its ministry as equipping all of its people for ministry in the world, the seminaries would become scenes of tremendous excitement.

The way is clear to liberate the *laos*. It must begin with the laity unlocking the doors of their own prisons of religious institutionalism and claiming their ministry in the world. It must be supported by professional church leaders who have caught the vision of God acting in today's world through the laity. Working together, the *laos* can thus shift the focus of the national church, its seminaries, districts, and congregations from seeing our religious institutions as ends in themselves to seeing them as a means to an end. The *laos* can and must be liberated for ministry in the world.

NOTES—CHAPTER 15

1. *The Dogmatic Constitution of the Church,* Paragraph 31.
2. Christopher Walters-Bugbee, "Across the Great Divide: Seminaries and the Local Church," *The Christian Century* (November 11, 1981).
3. Hendrick Kraemer, *A Theology of the Laity* (Philadelphia: Westminster Press, 1958).
4. Ibid.

Epilogue

It is not my expectation that after reading this book we will be able to say, "Thank God, it's Monday!" with the same degree of enthusiasm that we thank him for Friday. The Monday world is a difficult one, full of ambiguities and dilemmas. We are constantly barraged with a worldly theology that equates our worth with our works, and so we are never at peace with ourselves. We feel we are the victims of systems and organizations over which we have no control. It is no wonder we are happy to be freed, if only for a few days, from such a world, and we can truly thank God, it's Friday.

But there is no reason for Christians to feel powerless to deal with the Monday world. The gospel has freed us from the need to measure up to worldly success. The life of Jesus has demonstrated that no earthly principality or power can have dominion over us. The Bible affirms that there is purpose in life for us.

The apostle Paul had enough struggles, hardships, imprisonments, and disputes to fill the lives of ten people. Yet he had the assurance that he was not the captive of any earthly power. He was not a Pollyanna; he freely admitted to his problems. But they never overcame him. He wrote, "We are afflicted in every way, but not crushed; perplexed, but not driven to despair" (2 Cor. 4:8).

It is in the Monday world that God's creative process continues daily. It is in the Monday world that God has called us to do productive work. It is in the Monday world that the hungry can be fed, the sick restored to health, and the dispossessed given homes. The Monday world is where God's concern for love and justice is demonstrated. It is the Monday world which gives purpose to our lives.

As God's priests, our parish is the Monday world.

As Christians, we should be able to "Thank God, it's Monday!"

196